THE HEADSTONE DETECTIVE AGENCY

OTHER MYSTERIES BY ROBERT J. RANDISI

Hitman with a Soul Trilogy
Upon My Soul
Souls of the Dead
Envy the Dead

The Johnny Headston Series
The Headstone Detective Agency
Headstone's Folly (*)
A Headstone for Hire (*)

The Miles Jacoby Series
Eye in the Ring
The Steinway Collection
Full Contact
Separate Cases
Hard Look
Stand Up

The Nick Delvecchio Series
No Exit from Brooklyn
The Dead of Brooklyn
The End of Brooklyn

The Gil & Claire Hunt Series
Murder is the Deal of the Day
The Masks of Auntie Laveau
Same Time, Same Murder

The Joe Keough Series
Alone with the Dead
In the Shadow of the Arch
Blood on the Arch
East of the Arch
Arch Angels
Back to the Arch

The Dennis McQueen Series
The Turner Journals
Cold-Blooded

The Rat Pack Series
Everybody Kills Somebody Sometime
Luck be a Lady, Don't Die
Hey You, with the Gun in Your Hand
You're Nobody til Somebody Kills You
I'm a Fool to Kill You
Fly Me to the Morgue
It was a Very Bad Year
You Make Me Feel So Dead
The Way You Die Tonight
I Only Have Lies for You

The Auggie Velez/Nashville Series
The Honky Tonk Big Hoss Boogie
The Last Sweet Song of Hammer Dylan
The Festival of Death

Stand Alone Crime Novels
The Disappearance of Penny
The Ham Reporter
Curtains of Blood
The Offer
The Bottom of Every Bottle
The Picasso Flop

Collections
Delvecchio's Brooklyn
The Guilt Edge

(*) – Coming Soon

ROBERT J. RANDISI

THE HEADSTONE DETECTIVE AGENCY

A John Headston P.I. Novel

DOWN&OUT
BOOKS

Down & Out Books
3959 Van Dyke Road, Suite 265
Lutz, FL 33558
DownAndOutBooks.com

Cover design by Zach McCain

ISBN: 1-64396-032-6
ISBN-13: 978-1-64396-032-6

On my headstone it will say,
"The best thing I ever did was to love Marthayn."

CHAPTER ONE

It is better to have been successful, and lost, than never to have been successful at all?

Bullshit!

In 1998 The Headstone Detective Agency had a dozen operatives working for me, thirty-year-old Johnny Headston.

In 2018 the Headstone Detective Agency consisted of one operative...fifty-year-old me.

I had handled a couple of big cases early in my career, which brought me attention and money, so I was able to open my office on Fifth Avenue in Manhattan. I began hiring operatives, grew to an eleven-man and one-woman staff, until the bottom fell out. (More on that later).

These days I'm still the Headstone Detective Agency, but now I'm down to a staff of one—me! I'm still in the same space—eighteenth floor of 580 Fifth Avenue—with empty desks stretched out across the floor, but that's because my office is rent-controlled. Even if I moved somewhere with a quarter of the space, my going rate would more than double. And these days, even rent-controlled, is a struggle.

That morning I was pounding the cyber-pavement, looking for work, posting my services on the web through

Facebook, Twitter, LinkedIn and any other service I could manage to understand, when my phone rang.

I kept a landline for business purposes, even though I carried my cell phone with me everywhere. When I was out of the office, I simply had the calls forwarded to my cell. But this was the landline ringing, which was encouraging.

"Headstone Agency," I said into the phone. It was still the best way to let people know they had dialed the right number. Nothing fancy like "How may I help you?" or "How may I direct your call?" There was no call directing. I was it.

"I—I hope I have the right number," a woman's voice said, timidly.

"I'm sure you do, ma'am," I said. "What can I do for you?"

"Well...I was going to come to your office, but I live in Westchester County."

It would have been a train ride into the city, but I said, "We can do this over the phone, ma'am. Just tell me what the problem is."

"Is this Mr. Headstone?"

"The name is Headston," I said, "but the agency is called Headstone. It's sort of a play—yes, I'm John Headston."

"The private detective?"

So okay, this was going to be like pulling teeth.

"That's right."

"Mr. Headstone, would it be possible for you to come here? To my house? I prefer to do business is person. I like to look into the eyes of people I do business with."

While her tone of voice was still rather timid, her manner really wasn't. And she still had the name wrong.

Westchester County, I thought. There would probably be money involved. And by that, I mean, serious money.

"Let me have your address, ma'am," I said, grabbing some paper and a pen. "Would this afternoon be convenient?"

"Yes, Mr. Headstone," she said, "that would be very convenient."

I hung up without correcting her.

I took the Metro-North to Westchester County, and Lyfted my way from the station to the home of Mrs. Nancy Kessenger. Even twenty years ago when I started it would have been the home of Mr. and Mrs. Templeton Kessenger, but things had changed in more ways than one.

It was a typical White Plains mansion, where many of Manhattan's elite commuted from each day. I knocked on the door, almost expected it to be answered by a General Sternwood black butler with white gloves, a la Chandler's *The Big Sleep*, but I was surprised when the lady herself answered the door.

"Ah, Mr. Headstone," she said, looking past me. "Your car?"

"It's Headston, ma'am, and I use Lyft these days," I told her. "Doesn't everyone? Saves me on speeding and parking tickets."

"I suppose. Come in, please."

She was a tall, willowy woman in her forties, who's only resemblance to General Sternwood was the stern look on her face. She wore white pants, and a short-sleeved pale blue silk blouse. From the condition of her arms my guess was she spent a lot of time on the country club tennis courts.

"Please close the door and follow me. We can talk in the den."

I did as she asked and trailed behind her through the large house, which seemed to have mostly tiled, shiny floors.

The den was done in maroon and green, with overstuffed furniture and overstuffed bookshelves.

"Can I offer you something?" she asked. "A drink, perhaps."

"A little early for me," I said, feeling underdressed in my best suit.

"Coffee, then?"

I had smelled coffee when I entered, and there was a pot in the corner, so I said, "That would be fine."

She poured two china cups and handed me one, complete with the saucer. I almost expected cookies, but there were none.

"Please, have a seat," she said.

I sat in one of the maroon chairs, and she chose one of the green ones. It was warm in the room, but certainly not as hot as General Sternwood's hothouse. (Okay, I'm done with the Chandler references.)

"I'm not comfortable with this," she said, "so I suppose I'll just blurt it out."

"In your own time," I invited.

"My husband is missing."

And she couldn't have told me that over the phone?

CHAPTER TWO

"He left for work several days ago and hasn't returned."

"Did you call the police?"

"Yes, apparently this sort of thing happens all the time. They suggested I call back in forty-eight to seventy-two hours. I—I couldn't wait that long."

She looked around, spotted what she wanted and took a cigarette from a box on a nearby table. It was one of the smokeless kind, but these days they say those'll kill you just as easily. She didn't ask if I minded, but then it was her house.

"But you did wait two days."

"I...thought he might come home last night."

"Has he done this before?"

"He's come home late before, but not...not days."

"Well, you might consider calling the police again."

"I will," she said, "but I'd like you to get started looking for him, Mr. Headston."

"Okay." I didn't tell her that I would probably have to check in with the White Plains detectives, just to safeguard my license.

"Where does he work?" I took out my notebook. I should have been using a tablet, but I wasn't that progressive, yet.

"Wall Street."

"A brokerage house, or a bank?"

"Brokerage house. Herman James."

Herman James was one of New York's top brokerage firms. Kessenger must have been a top-notch wheeler dealer to be working for them.

"Have you called his office, talked to his secretary? His boss?"

"Yes, and yes," she said. "Today's Wednesday. He left for work Monday. They say he showed up that morning, but later in the afternoon they couldn't locate him. And they haven't seen him since."

That was going to be my first stop, when I got back to Manhattan. I had to make this trip to White Plains worth it.

"I'll need a photo," I said. "One you won't mind if I don't give back to you."

"No problem."

"And I'll need a retainer."

"I expected that." It sounded like she was judging me, but I didn't care.

"Let me ask a few more questions, and then you can get me those things," I suggested.

"All right."

"How's your marriage?"

She hesitated, then said, "Convenient."

"Is the romance gone?"

"If you knew Templeton you wouldn't ask that," she said. "There was no romance to begin with."

"Could he be seeing another woman?"

"He could," she said, "but I doubt it."

"Are you seeing another man?"

"No." There was no expression on her face, no inflection in her tone. This woman was very hard to read, but I had the feeling she was lying.

"Do you have any children?"

"No, we've never had children."

"How long have you been married?"

"Twenty years."

"Could this be some sort of reaction to that?" I asked. "What I mean is, perhaps some kind of a midlife crisis? How old is he?"

"He's forty-five," she said, thoughtfully, "and you might be right. But when that happens don't men usually buy a new car, or stray?"

"Those are the usual signs," I said. "Has he changed his hair, his hygiene habits? Maybe lost some weight?" All the things a man having an affair would do.

"None of that."

"Has he gotten quiet? Moody?"

"He's always quiet."

"Does he have an office here in the house?"

"Yes."

"Can you show it to me?"

"Of course." She didn't get up.

"Now?" I said.

"Oh, yes." This time she stood up. "If you'll follow me, please."

I followed her to a central staircase, and up. Her pants were tight, and I followed what I was dead sure was a tennis or Pilates shaped butt up the stairs.

She took me down a plush carpeted hallway to an open doorway, then stood aside and gestured for me to enter ahead of her.

"This is his office," she said.

It looked like a model office, with a desk, a chair, a

file cabinet and some bookshelves. What made it look even more like a model was that it appeared unused. There were no papers on top of the desk, nothing was out of place by even an inch.

I walked around, opened the desk drawers, the file cabinets. The usual stuff was there, pens, paper clips, file folders. I also noticed there was no dust.

In one drawer I found a stack of phone bills that showed his carrier was AT&T. That was good. A friend of mine had shown me how to get AT&T records on my computer. Not legal, but helpful.

"I'm gonna take one of these," I said, grabbing the top bill and showing it to her.

"Take whatever you need," she said.

"Do you have a cleaning woman?" I asked, pocketing the bill.

"Yes."

"And she comes in here?"

"Yes, she does."

I looked at the books on the shelves. One whole section was fiction, and another nonfiction.

"Did he do much work in here?"

"I don't know," she said.

I looked at her.

"He would come in here after dinner and close the door. I don't know what he did here."

"Mrs. Kessenger," I asked, "does your husband make a lot of money?"

"Mr. Headstone," she said, "you sound like you're from Brooklyn. Are you?"

"Born and raised," I said, not bothering to correct her. Sometimes you've just got to let things go. And as long as she signed the check…

"Well then, you'll understand this very well," she said. "My husband makes a shitload of money."

CHAPTER THREE

We went back downstairs to the den.

"What staff do you have in the house?"

"The maid, and the cook."

"Both women?"

"Yes."

"Young?"

"No. If you have visions of a nubile young girl in a French maid's costume, you're mistaken. Both of them are older than I am."

I had the feeling she had made sure of that when she hired them.

"Do you belong to a country club?"

"Yes."

"Both of you?"

"Templeton rarely goes," she said. "I use the facilities for tennis, Pilates, that sort of thing. And to take lunch."

"Take" lunch, not "have" lunch. People with money talk differently.

"Can you get me that photo now, Mrs. Kessenger?"

"Yes, of course. I'll just be a moment."

While she was gone, I strolled the den, looked at books on the shelves there. The titles meant nothing to me, it didn't seem as if there were any novels. And then I noticed they were color coordinated. All of the spines were either maroon or green. This was a room where nobody ever touched the books. They were there for show.

She returned with a five-by-eight photo that looked like it had come from Sears. Templeton Kessenger appeared very distinguished, hair dark except for some grey at the temples, a face that would be called handsome if it weren't for the fact that his eyes were kind of beady. Or maybe he was just so unhappy in the photo that it showed.

"How old is this?"

"A couple of years."

I turned it over and looked at the back. It was blank. I was tempted to fold it in half in front of her and put it in my pocket, but I thought I'd save that for later.

"Is there anything else you can think to tell me?" I asked. "Does he have male friends? Buddies? Was he ever in the armed forces?"

"No to all of that," she said. "He is a quiet, conservative man who keeps to himself, even from me."

"So this disappearance comes as a complete surprise."

"Oh, yes," she said. "Templeton leaves home every day, returns home every day. Like clockwork. This is...well, a shock."

From where I stood, I could see out the window. There was a man working in the garden.

"You said you only had a maid and a cook as staff?" I asked.

"That's right."

"What about that guy?" I pointed out the window.

She looked, then said, "Oh, that's the gardener. I'm sorry, I didn't think of him. He's not here every day."

"Does he deal with you or your husband when he

gets paid, or takes instructions?"

"Usually me."

I walked to the window and looked out. He was bare-chested, young and in good shape. It made me wonder.

"What about a pool boy? Do you have one?"

"What? No, we don't have a pool."

"Chauffer?"

"No, I drive myself."

"So no other staff that you forgot to tell me about?"

"No."

"All right, then," I said. "I've got enough to get started. Uh, we did talk about a retainer."

She was ready with a check, which she held out to me. It had enough zeroes on it to make me happy.

"Thank you." I put it in my pocket.

"I'll see you out."

She walked me to the front door and opened it for me.

"Can I call you a cab?" she offered.

"That's okay," I said. "I have my cell. I'll call Lyft."

"Then I hope to hear from you soon."

"One more thing," I said, before she closed the door.

"Yes?"

"Would you call his office and tell someone I'm coming?"

"Yes, I'll do that."

"Thank you."

She closed the door and I went back down the walk. Before taking out my cell I decided to walk around to the side of the house and have a talk with the young gardener.

He was right where I had seen him, hacking away at some bushes with a pair of shears. As he worked both hands the muscles in his arms bunched and jumped. He looked all of twenty-three or twenty-four, and I was sure he spent plenty of time in the gym.

"Excuse me?" I said.

He stopped what he was doing and stared at me.

"I'd like to ask you some questions—"

He took me totally by surprise when he dropped the shears, turned and ran.

CHAPTER FOUR

"Mr. Headstone," she said, surprised to see me when she opened the door this time.

"Mrs. Kessenger," I said, "can you tell me why your gardener would run from me rather than answer any questions?"

"Oh my, he ran?"

"Yes, he did," I said. "I didn't even get a chance to tell him who I was or what I wanted. Why would he do that?"

"Well...Joe's an ex-con. That may have something to do with it."

"I guess. Joe who?"

"His name is Joseph Valeria," she said. "I hired him through the country club. They said they were doing a program to help ex-cons get work."

"Do you have his address?"

"No, but the club would. Why do you want his address?"

"I only wanted to ask him a question or two about your husband," I said. "Get somebody else's perspective on his state of mind."

"I told you, they don't interact."

"Be that as it may, I'd like to know why he ran."

14

"He probably thought you were a policeman."

"I tell you what," I said. "When you see him, tell him to call me. If he does that, I won't pursue him."

"A-all right, I'll tell him...if I see him."

She had been hugging herself the whole time we talked about Joe, as if she was cold. I thought it was more a hug of guilt. Was there some cliché sex going on between the young gardener and the lady of the house?

"What's the name of your country club?" I asked. "Before I go back to the city, I guess I should check with them."

"By the time you get back to Manhattan, Wall Street might be closed."

"That's okay," I said. "I can start there bright and early tomorrow morning."

"All right," she said, and told me the name of the place, and where it was.

I took another Lyft to the Plains Valley Country Club, but this time made arrangements for him to come back and get me.

The first place I went to was the office of the manager of the place. I had to ask directions and walk a few miles of hallways before I reached it. The young lady at the reception desk looked at me like I was a Fuller Brush salesman. (Don't remember those? Neither did she, but that's how she was looking at me.)

"Can I help you?" From the cut of my suit she knew I wasn't there to apply for membership.

"I'd like to see the manager, please."

"Do you have an appointment?"

"No, I don't," I said, "but I'm sure Mrs. Kessenger

called ahead to tell him I was coming." The last thing I did before leaving was to ask her to do that.

"I'll check," she said, and picked up her phone. But she didn't dial. She looked at me for a few seconds, then said, "Would you sit over there, please?"

There were some uncomfortable looking metal-and-cushion chairs off to one side. They obviously didn't want people camping out. I went and sat. The metal arms of the chair were cold.

I watched as she spoke into the phone, glanced over at me a few times, then spoke again. Finally, she hung up.

"Mr. Chase will see you now, sir," she called out to me. Pointing behind her she added, "Right through that door."

"Thank you." I wanted to say something smart and snotty, but she had already forgotten I was there.

I knocked and entered.

The office was a lot better furnished than the reception area. Plush chairs, a large, oak desk with a big, broad-shouldered man behind it. Again, I thought about cliché sex, this time between a manager and a member's wife. Come on, the woman kept herself in shape for somebody, and it wasn't hubby.

He stood up and buttoned the jacket of his sharp sports coat before he extended his hand.

"Blackwell Chase," he said. "Folks around here just call me Blackie."

I shook his hand. "Hello, Blackie. I'm John Headston. I believe Mrs. Kessenger called—"

"Yes, she did," he said, "but she said your name was Headstone."

"That's the name of my agency." I handed him a card. "My last name is Headston."

16

"Well," he said, "I can see where she erred. Why don't you have a seat, Mr. Headston."

"Thanks."

I sat in the well-cushioned visitor's chair, and he sat back in his huge leather swivel chair—pausing, of course, to unbutton the jacket.

"Nancy called and explained her dilemma," he said. "She can't find Temp?"

I wondered if they were "Blackie" and "Temp" when they were face-to-face?

"Apparently," I said. "She says he left for work Monday and never came home."

"But today's Wednesday."

"She thought he might show up last night."

"Did she call the police?"

"Yes, but they're not prepared to take action just yet."

"I see," he said, folding his hands in front of him. "Well, how can I help?"

"Have you seen him in the past two days?"

"No."

"Could he have spent the night here?"

"I doubt it, but I can check." He picked up the phone and told somebody named Tiffany—probably the girl out front—to check on it. "Shouldn't take long," he promised me, hanging up.

"Mrs. Kessenger told me she comes here more than he does," I said.

"That's true," he said. "She comes for lunch, and to use the facilities. On occasion, I'll see Temp here with her for dinner."

"Does he ever come without her?"

"No." He was very definite about that.

"Does he play tennis? Golf?"

"No."

"Tell me, Mr. Chase," I said, "what do you think the chances are he's having an affair?"

"Temp?" Now he laughed. "Oh, no, no, not Temp."

"What makes you so positive?"

"Well, he's just...not the type. He's not exactly what you'd call a sexual beast." He leaned forward. "Look, I can take you outside this office and point out six members who are probably having an affair. Or are likely to."

"But not Mr. Kessenger."

"No, never, nuh-uh." He sat back again.

The phone rang. He picked it up, listened, and then said, "Thanks, doll." He hung up. "Nope, he wasn't here Monday or Tuesday night."

"Okay, then," I said. "I, uh, might want to talk to some of your members."

"You can do that," he said, "but Temp doesn't have any friends, here."

"Enemies?"

"Oh, no," he said, "that's not what I meant. He just hasn't spent enough time with any of our members for them to be either."

"I see." I stood up, and he followed, buttoning his jacket before we shook hands. "Well, thank you for your time."

"Sure," he said, "anything I can do, don't hesitate to call on me. I like Nancy and Temp."

I had the feeling he liked Nancy a whole lot better. Maybe he, himself, was a sexual beast.

CHAPTER FIVE

Lyft was waiting for me when I got outside the gates. I'd decided not to talk to any of the members, not just yet. I had two other options I needed to pursue first.

There was still time for me to get back to the city and to Wall Street before it closed, especially if I had Lyft take me all the way there, instead of to the train. On the other hand, just as I had done with the country club, I was already out here, so I might as well go to the White Plains police and get that over with. At the moment, I wasn't working one of their active cases. It would be a courtesy for me to stop in and see them, which might go a long way later.

In the end I asked the Lyft driver if he knew where the police station was. He did. I told him to take me there.

Apparently, the City of White Plains did not have a Police Department or a Sheriff's Office, they had a Law Department. It was located on Main Street. The man I spoke with was a police officer, not a detective.

He checked his records and said, "No, we don't have a record of anyone by that name reported missing."

"Well, he wasn't officially reported. His wife called,

but nobody would take a report."

"Then why are you here?"

"Just to touch base and tell you that I'm looking for him."

"You're looking for a guy who's not missing."

"No, he is missing, just not according to you."

"Mister," the cop said, "it's according to us that counts. Now, if you wanna spend your time looking for a guy who isn't missin', be my guest. We don't care."

I decided not to frustrate myself any further.

"Fine. Thanks for your time."

"Sure thing."

Outside I asked the Lyft driver if he'd take me to Manhattan.

"Well...sure."

"Is that going to affect my Lyft rating?" I asked.

"I guess that'll depend on how you tip," he said.

I tipped him well. I wanted my rating to stay good, maybe a four out of five. I have a driver's license and I'll rent a car when it's absolutely necessary, but Lyft is a nice contrast to New York's Yellow Cabs, gypsy cabs and car services.

We made it to Wall Street by 3:50 p.m. As far as I knew, trading hours ended at 4 p.m. But I assumed the offices of Herman James would be open until five. An elevator ride would tell me if my assumption was right.

The offices of Herman James took up two floors, twelve and fourteen (yes, that's right, no thirteenth floor). Judging from the directory in the lobby, it looked like management was on the fourteenth floor, so that's where I went.

People were traveling the hallway, walking swiftly in both directions, carrying papers. I wondered if it was this way every day near closing of the market.

I walked along the hall, which was lined with office doors. At one end sat a girl at a desk behind double glass doors. On the door was written Herman James & Associates. I squared my shoulders, sucked in my gut, but there was nothing I could do about my suit. It was a dead giveaway.

I went through the door and stopped in front of her desk. She was expertly made up. Blood-red lipstick was made even bloodier by her pale skin. I waited, but she didn't bother looking up at me or inquiring if she could help.

"Hello?" I said. I waved my hand in front of her face. "Do you see me?"

She looked up with a bored expression and asked, "Yes?"

"I'd like to see whoever's in charge."

"Of what?"

"Of the company."

"You'll have to tell me what it's about so I can find the appropriate person and then check if they have time to see you."

"I don't suppose there's a Herman James?"

"Not anymore."

"Uh-huh," I said. "Okay, then I'd like to speak to Templeton Kessenger's boss."

She stared at me for a few seconds, and then said, "Oh. Uh, what's your name?"

"John Headston. I'm here representing Mrs. Kessenger."

"Just wait." She picked up her phone, covered it with

her mouth and had a conversation with somebody. The only word I caught was "Headstone." When she hung up, I swore there was lipstick on the receiver.

"Please wait, someone will be right out."

"Do you know Mr. Kessenger?"

"Only because he walks past me every morning."

"But not today or yesterday, right?"

"Right."

"Did he walk past you on Monday?"

"Yes, he did."

"And did he walk past you when he left Monday?"

"No," she said. "By the time I left he hadn't gone yet."

"But he was still here then?"

She hesitated. "I don't know."

"Why not?"

"Well, I didn't see him go out for lunch, or come back. But that might've been because I was out to lunch."

"I get it." He could've gone and returned while she was out, or he could have gone to lunch and not come back. Or maybe he didn't go to out, at all. I wondered how hard it would be to get rid of a body up here.

I looked to my right, saw a young man walking up the hall towards us, wearing a grey suit and a perfect haircut. As he got closer, I could see that he was probably all of twenty-four or five years old.

"Mr. Headstone?"

"Headston," I said, "but that's close enough."

He continued as if I hadn't spoken.

CHAPTER SIX

"Will you follow me, please?"

He turned to walk back the way he had come and didn't bother to turn and check to see if I was, indeed, following him. Only when he reached the door he wanted did he turn.

"Right in here. You'll be seeing Mr. Scott Walcott. He's the managing partner of the firm."

"Fine."

He opened the door and ushered me in.

I didn't notice the man behind the desk right away because of the panoramic view of the city through the window behind him. When I did look at him, he was staring at me, expectantly. He seemed to be in his mid-forties with thinning hair and a growing middle. I knew the feeling.

"Sorry," I said, "but that view…"

He turned his head to briefly look, then turned back toward me and said, "Spoils of war."

Meaning he was the victor. I got it.

"Mr. Headstone, what can I do for you? You said this had to do with Temp Kessenger?"

"Yes," I said. "His wife has hired me to find him. And the name is Headston."

"Oh, sorry. So he *is* missing, then?"

"Apparently." Although, I added to myself, not as far as the police are concerned.

"Please, have a seat."

We both sat.

"We were wondering what happened when he didn't show up for work either Tuesday or today."

"What about Monday?"

"He was here."

"Yes, but did he stay all day? Or did he go to lunch and never come back? Your receptionist doesn't seem sure."

"My feeling is he went to lunch and didn't return," Walcott said. "We had a staff meeting later that day and he wasn't there."

"Should he have been?"

"Temp is more than staff," Walcott said. "He's a partner."

"Really?" Mrs. Kessenger hadn't told me that. "Mr. Walcott, how much is he worth? Personally, I mean?"

"Didn't Nancy tell you?"

"She didn't tell me he was a partner, she only told me he makes, and I quote 'a shitload of money.'"

He smiled briefly.

"I don't know his exact personal worth," he said, "but it's probably north of twenty million."

So he could be anywhere, I thought. I made a mental note to ask Mrs. Kessenger to check her bank accounts and see if any large withdrawals had been made.

"Tell me," I said, "are you friends?"

"Even if we started out as friends," Walcott said, "being partners tends to change that."

"So you're not."

"We don't hang out together, if that's what you mean."

"And did you start this company together?"

"We did."

"Who's Herman James?"

"There's no Herman James. It's just a name. We had to call it something and Kessenger and Walcott didn't have a ring to it."

"Would you know if he has a place he's always wanted to go?"

"I don't get you."

"You know," I said, "a fantasy, like Tahiti or Barbados. Everyone has one, don't they?" Mine was Vegas, but that's another story.

"No," he said, "Temp's never talked about anything like that. He was always living in the present."

"I get the impression he was all work and no play."

"Exactly."

"No sense of humor?"

"None."

"His wife doesn't think he was cheating."

"Oh, no," he said, "not Temp." He sounded just like "Blackie."

"Did he not like women?" I asked. "And sex?"

"Are you asking me if he's gay?"

"No, no," I said, "but I got the impression from his wife that they hadn't been intimate in some time."

"Temp had other things on his mind."

"What about his wife?"

"Nancy? What about her?"

"Does she cheat?"

"If she does it's not with me," he said. "I don't think I've seen Nancy in...months."

"How long have they lived in Westchester County?"

"Temp bought that house...oh, a dozen years or so ago."

"Does he have any friends here, in the firm?"

"No," Walcott said, "like I said, he always has other things on his mind."

"Business over friends or women?"

"Exactly."

"Does he have an office like this?"

"Indeed he does."

"May I see it?"

"Sure," he said, picking up the phone, "I'll have Daniel show you—no, you know what?" He hung up and stood. "I'll walk you over there, myself."

He strode past me and I hurried to keep up with him. Standing in front of that view I hadn't noticed how tall he was. He had to be six-two or three and took long strides. I tried not to run to keep up.

CHAPTER SEVEN

Templeton Kessenger had a corner office.

I'd been in enough office buildings to know that corner offices were a prize. It seemed to me that Kessenger had gotten the true "spoils of war," here, which might explain why the two ex-friends were now only partners.

"Wow, pretty snazzy," I said. Even the furnishings were more upscale than those in Walcott's office.

"Temp liked nice things."

We had passed a pretty woman on the way in, sitting at a desk.

"And the girl outside? Is she his secretary?"

"She is."

"Can we get her in here so I can ask her a few questions?"

"Sure, I'll get her."

While he stepped outside, I went over behind Kessenger's desk and looked out the window at his view. I could clearly see the street below. Make out names of the stores and restaurants, including something I didn't expect to see on Wall Street—a Burger World.

I turned as Walcott reentered with the secretary trailing. She looked to be in her twenties, kept her head down and her hands folded in front of her. She was sedately dressed in a blouse buttoned to her neck and a skirt that covered her knees. She wore a minimum of make-up.

"This is Ally, Temp's administrative assistant," Walcott said. "Ally, this is Mr. Headston. He's a detective looking for your boss." Walcott turned to me. "I'll leave you two alone. You can stop by my office on your way out."

"I'll find it," I said. "Thanks."

He nodded, patted Ally on the arm and left.

As the door closed, the girl's entire posture changed. She unfolded her hands, lifted her chin so she could look at me, and rolled her eyes.

"What a tool!"

"That bad?" I asked.

She rolled her eyes again, then sat in her boss's visitor's chair.

"So you're a cop? You don't look like a cop."

"I'm not a cop," I said. "I'm private."

"A P.I.?" she asked, her eyes widening. "Cool!"

"You mind if I sit here?" I asked, indicating her boss's chair.

"I don't care," she said. "Is he comin' back?"

"I hope so," I said, sitting, "as soon as I find him. Do you have any idea where he is?"

"Me? Hell, no," she said. "All I do is answer his phone."

"Does he ever get calls from women?"

"Women clients," she said. "If you mean women for, like, sex...ew!"

"I've been told he wasn't interested in sex."

"Geez, no," she said. "He never made a move on me. But why would he, when I'm dressed like this?"

"You don't dress like this outside of work?"

"Hell, no. Dig this." She unbuttoned her top two buttons and opened her blouse, revealing a snake tattoo that went around her neck. "If they knew I had this they'd fire me."

"Against company policy?"

"Yuh." She buttoned up again.

"That and the skirt at the knees?"

"Yup."

I noticed she was wearing flat shoes.

"And in high heels?"

"They'd prefer not," she said, in a very proper tone.

"What about the receptionist?" I asked. "The one with all the make-up and red lipstick."

"If you check Walcott's dick," she said, "you'll find a red circle around the base. She sets the women's lib movement back to the Mad Men fifties."

"Ah…"

"So, what's the deal with Mr. Kessenger?"

"He didn't go home," I said. "His wife's worried."

"Yeah, bet me," she drawled.

"She's not worried about him?"

"She's worried about the money."

"Do you know how much money your boss has?"

"No, but it's a boatload."

"What do you think of him?"

"He's all right."

"Not a tool?"

She rolled her eyes. "Not like that Walcott. Even though he's gettin' blowjobs from that vampire out front, he still makes time to try to squeeze my butt."

"Don't you report him?"

"To who? He's the boss. Besides, Rose McGowan I

ain't. And I don't intend to be around here for long."

"And Mr. Kessenger never did that?"

"Hell, no," she said. "He's all business all of the time."

"Do you like him?"

She shrugged. "He's okay. I've had worse bosses."

"Well, if you think of anything, maybe something he said or a phone call he got, I'll leave my card with you on the way out and you can call."

"Sure," she said, standing. "I hope you find him."

"I'm gonna look around in here a little while longer."

"Fine with me."

As she headed for the door my stomach grumbled.

"I don't suppose you could get somebody to go down to Burger World and bring me a world burger, could you?"

"Are you kiddin'?" she asked. "Nobody from this office ever goes to Burger World."

"Yeah, okay, thanks."

She went out and even before she was through the door, I could see that posture change again.

CHAPTER EIGHT

I went through his desk drawers without finding anything of interest. No travel brochures for Jamaica or Bali. No take-out menus. No phone numbers written on small slips of paper or matchbooks.

I went to the window again and looked out. My stomach was still grumbling, so whether anybody up here liked it or not, there was a burger in my future. And probably some onion rings, too.

I left the office, dropped my card off with the now sedate looking Ally, winked at her and went back down the hall. As I entered Walcott's outer office, I noticed again there was no secretary at the desk.

I knocked and went in.

"Is your girl gone for the day?" I asked.

"No girl," he said. "I fired her last week, haven't replaced her, yet."

"What'd she do?"

"It was what she didn't do."

"And what was that?" I asked, thinking of what Ally had told me.

"Her job."

Uh-huh.

"How do you get by without a secretary?"

"The receptionist out front comes in and helps me out."

Yeah, I bet.

"Mr. Walcott, who benefits if Mr. Kessenger never comes back?"

"I suppose his wife," he said. "The partnership agreement says his shares in the company go to her."

"So you don't benefit?"

"This company is a success because of Temp," Walcott said. "If he doesn't come back, I don't benefit, at all. None of us will."

"And if he dies?"

"I believe it's the same," he said. "Everything goes to her."

"And what happens if you die?"

"I don't have any family," Walcott said. "My shares would go to Temp. Wait, do you think Nancy killed him?"

"Well, the way your company is set up, it would make more sense for her to kill you before she kills him."

He thought about that a moment, then said, "Hey, you're right."

"So no, I guess I don't think she killed him. At least, not yet."

"I better talk to our corporate attorney," he commented, looking concerned.

"I guess that wouldn't be a bad idea," I said. "But if I was you, I'd wait until this is all over."

"Why?"

"If you make any changes now, it might look suspicious to the cops."

"Are the police involved?" he asked.

"Not yet," I said, "but they will be, at some point."

"Well…thank you for the advice," he said, "but I think I should at least call my lawyer."

"You do that," I replied, "and see what he says."

"And can you let me know if you find him?"

"Sure."

He picked up his phone.

"Let me leave you my card," I said, dropping one on the desk. "Your lawyer might want to know who I am."

"All right."

I started for the door, then stopped and turned.

"Mr. Walcott, the girl out front. With the red lipstick?"

"Jackie, yes?"

"She looks kind of…well, you know. Do you think she and Kessenger might have been, you know…"

"Oh, no," he said, "I can assure you that wasn't the case. Believe me, I'd know."

I smiled inside and said, "I bet you would."

CHAPTER NINE

On the street I had to get my bearings, figure out which side of the building Kessenger's office was so that I could locate Burger World. But I noticed a Subway right across the street from where I was, so rather than strain my brain, I crossed over.

I stayed simple and had a turkey and bacon sandwich. I didn't usually patronize Subway, because they require too much of a question-and-answer period before they give you a sandwich. What kind of bread? What kind of cheese? Do you want that microwaved? What else would you like on it? Would you like a bag of chips? What would you like to drink? Would you like a cookie?

"White bread, turkey, bacon, lettuce, that's it," I told the sandwich maker.

"What kind of bread?" she asked, because that's what she was trained to do.

It's the same when you go into a restaurant. Try counting the questions you have to answer before you can eat and you'll see what I mean.

I went in one day and said, "Table for one."

The hostess said, "How many?"

You can't skip over the minutiae in life, anymore. It's frustrating.

I took my sandwich and Coke and sat down at a table in an upstairs dining room. I was able to look down at the street from the window. The Wall Streeters were starting to hit the street, heading home. I had already had a full day, myself. A trip to Westchester to talk with the wife, the club and the cops, and back to the city to talk to the work colleagues. All I knew was that Templeton Kessenger seemed to have no interest in anything but work. Why then would he not have gone to his office on Tuesday or Wednesday?

By the time I had finished my sandwich and washed it down I realized who I hadn't talked to yet. I went back across the street and into the building.

In front of the wall directory was a security desk and a guard sitting at it. I showed him my I.D. and told him what I was doing.

"Buddy," he said, "there's a lot of floors in this building, and I'm a guard, not a doorman. There's only a few people I recognize on sight."

I took a long look at him. He was in his fifties. His face was a mass of broken capillaries, and his big nose was red.

"I'll bet you're an ex-cop."

"You got that right," he said. "Twenty years with the NYPD, poundin' a beat. You know what, they don't got beats no more."

"Things have changed."

"You said it."

"But I'll bet one thing hasn't."

"What's that?"

"Your instincts," I said. "I'll bet you know trouble when you see it come through the door."

"You got that right," he assured me.

"See, I'm wondering if my guy had any bad habits, like women or gambling. Have you seen anybody come through that front door lately who looks like a bookie, or an angry husband?"

"This building? Naw."

"Okay, so you don't know Mr. Kessenger by name," I said. "How about this?" I showed him the photo.

"Oh, yeah," the guard said, "him, I seen him...he comes in and out, but we don't ever, like, talk or anythin'. You know, some of these guys say hi, how are ya, see that game last night, but that's about it. This guy...nothin'."

"Okay." I took the picture back.

"Although...lemme see that again."

I gave it back. He studied it a little longer, then handed it to me.

"There's somethin' nigglin' at me, but...ah..."

"Maybe it'll come to you later," I said, giving him my card. "Call me if it does."

"Sure thing, bud."

I pocketed the picture and left the building.

Rent control not only gave me a place to work, but to live, as well. I had a small apartment in the West Village, where I'd been living for twenty years. Several attempts had been made to get me out, but legally I can stay as long as I want, so they're going to find my cold, dead body there one morning.

The Subway sandwich didn't hold me very long, and as I neared my apartment, I was sorry I hadn't gone to Burger World. So I detoured to the Waverly Diner on 6th and got a burger and fries to go.

At home I sat in my small kitchen and ate, washing it

down with one of two bottles of Stella Artois I had in my frig. As much as I liked the fries at some of the fast food places, there was nothing like thick cut, greasy diner fries.

I finished my meal and took the rest of my Stella to the small desk I kept in front of the window, my office away from office.

Other than having served some summonses earlier in the week for a lawyer who still threw work my way in spite of my checkered past, the Kessenger case was the only thing I was working on. So I sat and made notes from the first day of my investigation.

His wife had last seen him Monday morning, when he left for work; the people at Herman James had last seen him Monday, maybe when he left there for lunch; the people at the Country Club hadn't seen him in weeks.

Nobody thought he was cheating.

Everybody said he didn't have any friends.

I sat back and looked at my notes. What I was looking for was a man who had millions of dollars, a wife who didn't love him, no friends, no girlfriends, a partner who didn't seem to like him, and the only nice thing his secretary could think of to say about him was that he "wasn't a tool."

I hand-wrote my notes because, although I had a computer at my office, I refused to have one at home. I didn't want to take a chance I'd get hooked on porn sites or chat rooms—or both.

I watched some late night TV—movies, not talk shows—and then headed off to bed.

CHAPTER TEN

I entered my office carrying a container of coffee and two bagels in a paper bag. There was a good deli right around the corner from where the Brentano's bookstore used to be. Once upon a time booklovers could stroll 5th Avenue and stop into the numerous bookstores—three Doubledays, Brentanos, Scribners, Classics, B. Daltons, various other stores that carried books, among other things. These days we were limited to the Barnes & Noble on the corner of 49th Street.

Luckily, we still had some delis, even though we'd lost some biggies like the Carnegie and Stage (one-time nemesis in the Restaurant War), as well as the New York Deli. We still had lesser options, and infamous ones like the 2nd Avenue Deli and Katz's were still around if you wanted to take a subway ride, or a long walk.

I ate my breakfast while I turned on my computer, an aged HP that still worked, albeit slowly. First, I opened a Word file titled KESSENGER, and transcribed all the notes I'd written the night before. Then I did my thing with the AT&T site and managed to download (illegally) Kessenger's phone records. I printed it out and then sat back in my chair to study it. There were a lot of numbers and, of course, none meant anything to me. I could have just sat and called each to see who answered, but that was tedious, and there were other ways.

I had the phone number for Herman James, so I called and asked for Templeton Kessenger's line, hoping that Ally would pick up. She did. She answered in a cool, businesslike tone.

"Mr. Kessenger's line."

"Ally, this is John Headston."

"Who?"

"The private eye."

"Hey, the P.I. What's happenin', man?" The professional tone was gone, and suddenly she was a different kind of cool. "How's it hangin'?"

"It's, uh, it's good," I said. "Listen, I need your help."

"My help? What, findin' Mr. Kessenger?"

"That' right."

"Awesome! Whataya want me to do?"

"I have a list of numbers from his phone," I said. "I wondered if you'd meet me somewhere and take a look, tell me which ones you recognize, and who they belong to?"

"Sure, man, but..."

"What?"

"...this ain't some kinda scam to get me alone somewhere, is it? I mean, you didn't seem like a perv when I met you, but—"

"No, no," I said, "I'm not a perv. We can meet someplace public if you're worried—"

"Relax, Mr. Private Eye," she said. "I'm just yankin' your chain. Where d'ya wanna meet?"

"Well, not in your office," I said. "I don't want anybody to see you helping me."

"I need-a deliver some papers down around Union

Square," she said.

"You're making deliveries? Don't they use a messenger service?"

"I think they're tryin' ta gimme something to do before they decide to let me go."

"I get it."

"Ya wanna meet in front of the Strand Book Store?"

"That's good," I said. "We can go inside and browse and I can show you the list of numbers."

"They're lettin' me combine the delivery with lunch," she said. "I think they just don't want me gettin' underfoot, you know? My days are numbered there, unless you find Mr. Kessenger. And even then. I mean, that was just supposed to be a temporary thing for me, but Mr. Kessenger liked me and made me his AA."

"What time can we met?"

"Like, eleven-thirty?"

"Good, I'll buy you lunch instead of goin' in the Strand. There's a good little restaurant around the corner of twelfth."

"You gotta deal, P.I.," she said, and hung up.

CHAPTER ELEVEN

As Ally came walking up the street it took me a few minutes to recognize her. She looked very different from the girl who worked on Wall Street. She was totally sleeveless—yes, it was that warm, even in October—and her arms were covered with tattoos. Up in the office I had only seen the one around her neck, but now they were all on display. Some of the symbols were recognizable—an anchor, a wolf, some kind of astrological sign—and others were totally foreign.

"Stop starin'," she said, when she reached me.

"Sorry. You're a walking work of art."

"Aw, thanks, P.I.," she said. "Most people just think I'm fuckin' weird."

"What are you doing working on Wall Street?"

"I used to work in a tattoo parlor," she said. "Somebody came in for a tattoo and offered me a job. I took it. End of story. I guess that's gonna end if you don't find him."

"Kessenger?" I asked. "He came in for a tattoo?"

"Yep."

Maybe that was the beginning of a mid-life crisis.

"When?"

"A couple of months ago."

"Did he say why he wanted it?"

"No," she said, "just that he did."

"And he offered you a job?"

She nodded. "After I did the tattoo."

"What was it?"

"A wolf's head, on his right bicep."

"Did you think it was odd that he was there?"

"Oh, yeah," she said. "He stood out. There ain't many buttoned-down types who go for tattoos."

"So the you've been at Herman James for about two months?"

"Yes."

"And in that time, did he ever come on to you?"

"No. Why would he?"

"You're a pretty girl."

"Aw, P.I.," she said, "stop sayin' nice things to me."

"Why?"

"I ain't used to it. Weren't you gonna feed me?"

"Right, Let's go inside."

The place was a little no-name diner, looked like a hole-in-the-wall from outside, but inside it expanded.

"I've seen this place before," she said, when we were seated, "but never guessed all this was here."

"All this" was a lot of space with bare wood floors, wooden tables and chairs.

The menu was simple. I ordered a bowl of chili, which they served over white steamed rice. Ally had a turkey sandwich with fries.

"I've got this printout," I said, while we waited for our food. I passed it to her. "Do you know any of these numbers?"

"These are from his cell?" she asked.

"Yes."

"Well, I know a few of 'em," she said. "He's also called them from his HJ landline. But some of these others...can I keep this and get back to ya?"

"Of course," I said. "Anything you can come up with would be helpful."

"I'll let you know tonight, or tomorrow by the latest," she promised, folding the list and tucking it away.

"Great."

"So where d'ya think he is?" she asked.

"I don't know," I said. "I think he might be hiding from his wife."

"Why?"

"Because she seems to be someone a man would hide from."

"A bitch, you mean?"

"Cold," I said. "Have you met her? Spoken to her?"

"Once in a while she'll call the office," Ally said. "She never talks to me, just at me. 'Put him on,' that kind of thing. One day she called and said, 'Put that bastard on!'"

"Yeah, I guess I'd hide from her."

"So you think he's missin' because he wants to be?"

"I don't have any evidence that he's missing unwillingly," I said. "Can you tell me about enemies he has in business?"

"No," she said. "He's good at his job. As far as I can see, his clients are happy."

"What about his colleagues?" I asked. "He must be competing with somebody, up there."

"From what I could see in two months," she said, "he's a superstar. That company wouldn't be where it is without him, so why would anybody want him to disappear?"

"Okay," I said. "Thanks for that. I guess I'll assume

he's gone of his own volition."

"Why would you care what I have to say?" she asked.

"You're a smart lady," I said.

She stopped eating and stared at me.

"I should work for you," she said.

"What?"

"Yeah," she said, "whether he comes back or not, I should start workin' for you. You have a staff, right?"

"I have a staff," I said, "of one. I used to have a dozen, but that was a long time ago."

"What happened to them?"

It wasn't what happened to them, it was what happened to me, but I didn't want to go into that.

"They moved on," I said. "Some of them have their own agencies."

"Do you have a secretary?"

"No, not at the moment."

"There ya go," she said, grabbing her sandwich again, "I could be your secretary-slash-assistant."

"Let me get through this case, Ally," I said, "and then we'll see what happens."

"I'll give my notice," she said.

"Now hold on—"

"Relax, P.I.," she said. "I know what I wanna do."

"Yeah, but what about what I want to do?" I asked. "I couldn't pay you what you're worth, what you must be getting at Herman James—"

"Don't worry about it," she said. "It ain't always about the money, ya know. It's about what you're supposed to be doin'."

"Ally—"

"Eat your chili, P.I.," she said. "It's getting cold. Is that rice in there?"

CHAPTER TWELVE

Ally said she wasn't going to the Strand before heading back to work, but to the bookstore directly across the street from it, Forbidden Planet. It dealt in comics, graphic art, books, clothes, something called manga, and that was from what I could see outside. I'd never been inside.

"Thanks for lunch, P.I.," she said, as we left the diner and walked up to Broadway.

"Thanks for your input, Ally."

"Is your name really Headstone?" she asked.

"That's the name of my agency," I said. "My name's Headston."

"Oh, I get it!" she said. "That's kinda cool. What's your first name?"

"John."

"Johnny?"

"To very few people."

"Ya know what?" she asked. "I'm gonna keep callin' ya P.I."

"That suits me," I told her.

I watched her cross the street and enter the store, then started walking toward Union Square.

* * *

After spending time with Ally at lunch, my office felt a little more cavernous and emptier. The unoccupied bullpen desks stretched out ahead of me, seemingly for miles. Maybe it wouldn't hurt to have Ally sitting at one of them.

I went into my office and sat at my desk, took a few moments to add my notes from Ally to the file in my computer. Then I decided to give Mrs. Nancy Kessenger a call.

"Did you find him?" she asked, after I identified myself.

"Not yet," I said. "I've talked to people at the club, and at Herman James."

"You talked to Scottie?"

"Walcott, yes."

"He hates Temp."

"Isn't your husband the reason everybody at Herman James is making money?"

"Exactly," she said. "That's why Scottie hates him. And..." She stopped.

"And what?"

"And me," she said, after a few beats.

"Walcott's in love with you?"

"Always has been," she said.

"Well, that's one thing," I said. "Why would Walcott hate Temp for making their company a success?"

"Don't you know," she said, "that you hate the people who help you the most? Think about it. You see them when they're at their lowest, you help them get back up, and then they have to see you all the time and feel in-debted. It weighs on them, and you become what they hate."

I almost argued with her, but a couple of things

popped into my head from my past and I knew she was right.

"Mrs. Kessenger—"

"Nancy."

"Do you think Walcott might have done something to your husband?"

"No," she said. "He hates him, but he needs him, and that makes him hate him even more. But there's one thing Scottie hates even more than Temp."

"What's that?"

"The thought of failure."

"What about Blackie?"

"Black—Blackwell Chase? What about him?"

"Is he into you, too?"

"Blackwell's as queer as a—he's gay."

"Oh."

"Maybe he's into Temp," she offered.

Was that a joke? From this woman?

"Have you heard from your husband?"

"No."

"Have you heard from the cops?"

"The po—no, should I?"

"I'll be in touch, Mrs.—"

"Nancy."

"Nancy." I said and hung up.

CHAPTER THIRTEEN

I had a friend who used to be a stockbroker. He burned out on the job, and now he's homeless—except that he says everywhere is his home. Usually, he sits on a bench in Bryant Park, located on 6th Avenue behind the New York Public Library Main branch. The park was actually built on top of an underground space that houses the library's stacks. Although it's a public park, it's managed by the Bryant Park Corporation.

The main entrance is on 6th Avenue, between 40th and 42nd Streets. As I entered, I saw Jack was sitting on his bench, reading the financial pages rather than staring out at the expanse of well-manicured lawn in front of him. The corporation allowed him to stay there because he was never dressed like a homeless person. He was usually clean, and always sober. The other reason was, he was not averse to handing out advice and stock tips to people who knew enough to stop by and ask.

I walked over to sit next to him. To me he's Jack, but to others who come by to pick his brain, he's "King Jack."

"Hey, Jack."

He didn't look up from his pages. "Headstone."

"How've you been?"

"I'm fine." This time he looked at me. "You look tired. Stressed, even."

"A little of both. You look good, well-rested, relaxed."

"That's me," he said, glancing back down at his paper. "I know you're not here for stock tips, so what's on your mind?"

"Henry James," I said.

He knew I wasn't talking about the novelist.

"New York's version of Edward Jones," he said. "But not as big."

"They make money though, right?"

"For some people."

"What about Walcott and Kessenger?"

"Kessenger is the brains," Jack said. "Without him, Walcott would be working the floor."

"And he knows it?"

"Oh, yeah."

"And he doesn't hate him for it?"

"Oh, he hates him," Jack said, "but not for that."

So what Ally had told me was true. I was right, she was a smart girl to have picked all that up in two months on the job.

"Kessenger's missing," I said.

He stopped and looked at me.

"How long?"

"Since Monday."

"Who reported it?"

"Nobody," I said. "His wife hired me, but the cops aren't in on it, yet. Have you heard anything?"

"Not a word. Do you think he left on his own, or something's up?"

"I'm not sure," I said. "Apparently his wife benefits if he dies."

"She gets his part of the company?"

I nodded.

"Well, that certainly wouldn't be worth killin' him," he commented.

"Why not?"

"Because without him, the company wouldn't be worth as much."

"So you don't think his wife or his partner would kill him."

"Only if they wanted to cut off their noses to spite their faces," Jack said. "If he's dead you're gonna have to look elsewhere."

"First I've got to find out if he's alive or dead," I pointed out. "I'm hoping it's just some sort of mid-life crisis."

"Not a woman," Jack said, looking back at his paper. "Not according to what I hear about him."

"Gay?"

He shook his head.

"Asexual," he said. "Doesn't care, at all. It's all about business."

"Maybe he got tired of the business."

"That could very well be," Jack said. "Lord knows some of us do."

"If he's really gone, maybe there's an opening there for you to get back in the business."

He gave me a cold look.

"Bite your tongue." Back to the paper. "I'm very happy right here on my bench."

"Well, if you don't mind, I'll check back with you in a day or two, see if you've heard any news."

"I'll be here."

I didn't offer him any money because I knew he

didn't need it.

"See ya, Jack."

I stood up.

"Headstone."

He didn't look up from his paper.

CHAPTER FOURTEEN

As I left Bryant Park my cell phone rang.

"Headstone Agency," I said. The thing I really hate about cell phones is talking into them while I'm outside. It just seems unnatural. And I hate people who do it while walking. I always stop and step to one side—into a doorway, if I can.

"Headstone?"

"Yeah," I said, because eventually I just do that. What's the point of fighting it?

"This is Gibson."

"Who?"

"The guard you talked to on Wall Street in the Herman James building."

"Oh yeah," I said. "What's up?"

"You might wanna get over here."

"Why?"

"In the department we used to call it an 'interesting development.'"

"Can you tell me—"

"I gotta go," he said. "I'll see ya when ya get here."

"But wait—"

He hung up.

Well, I wasn't really sure what my next move was

going to be, anyway. I put the phone in my pocket and headed for the subway.

When I got to the building it was well after lunch. There wasn't that much foot traffic going in and out. My guard, who I knew was named Gibson, was at his station. When he saw me he waved enthusiastically.

"What's going on?" I asked.

"I went to Burger World for lunch," he said.

"Yeah."

"Nobody around here goes there. They're all too frou-frou for that."

"Okay," I said. "Are we getting to the point, Gibson?"

"Lemme see that picture again."

I took out the picture of Kessenger and passed it over.

"Yeah," he said, handing it back, "I think I saw him in Burger World."

"When?"

"A couple of hours ago."

"Are you sure?"

"No," he answered. "I said I think I did, but I thought it was worth calling ya."

"Yeah, it was," I said. "Thanks. I'll go and check it out."

"He might not be there, anymore."

That was what I was thinking, but I thanked him again and left the building. I walked around the corner, crossed over to stand in front of Burger World. I looked up, counted fourteen floors and figured I was looking at Kessenger's window.

Burger World was a good size, and even though it wasn't lunchtime, and the Wall Street types didn't frequent it, it was still doing a brisk business. I stepped inside the front door and looked around at the customers. I didn't see anybody who looked like Templeton Kessenger. Maybe I'd have to come back at noon the next day, and a few days after that, before Kessenger showed up again. But if he was in Burger World at lunchtime, where was he before and after that?

I wanted to stick around a while longer, so I decided to get a Coke. As I turned to go to the counter, I saw the two cashiers with their Burger World uniforms on. One was a woman, and the other a man who looked too old for the job. But that wasn't the shocking part.

The shocking part was that the cashier was Templeton Kessenger.

CHAPTER FIFTEEN

"Why didn't you tell me he was working there?" I demanded of Gibson.

"What? Workin' there? I didn't know that," the guard said. "He was wearin' street clothes when I saw him. Maybe he just got there for his shift."

That could've been true. I bought a Coke before I left, but from the girl behind the counter. I got a closer look at Kessenger that way, to confirm it was really him, and also asked the girl when her shift ended.

"I'm gonna be here all night," she told me, thinking I was asking her out. "Sorry, Dad."

The "Dad" didn't hurt. After all I was fifty years old.

I assumed if a shift had just started, it might be Kessenger's, and I'd found him. He was working in Burger World. He didn't know I was there to find him, so there was no reason for him not to be there the next day.

"Are you sure that nobody from Herman James goes to Burger World?" I asked Gibson.

"I have never seen anybody come in here with a Burger World bag," he told me. "I've even had people comment while I'm sittin' here munchin' on fries."

"So none of his coworkers have seen him working there," I said. "Jesus. He's been right across the street the whole time."

"How long has he been workin' there?" Gibson asked.

"I don't know," I said. "I'd have to ask either him, or maybe the manager. Yeah, that's what I'll do. I'll talk to the manager about him."

"What if he sees you doin' that?" Gibson asked, like a cop. "Or what if the manager tells him? Won't he take off?"

"I don't think so," I said. "I mean, if he's hiding from everyone, why do it right across the street."

"Why would he leave Herman James and go to Burger World?"

"I don't know," I said, "but his secretary said she'd catch him staring out the window, down at the street. Could be he was staring at Burger World."

"And thinkin', 'Man, I'd like to work there?'"

"Who knows?" I said. "There's sure a lot less stress in that job."

"So, what're you gonna do?" he asked. "Talk to the guy, or just tell his wife where he is?"

"I haven't decided yet," I said. "I might just follow him home, see where he's living, so if I tell his wife I can toss that in, too."

"If you tell 'er?" he asked. "Why wouldn't ya? I mean, that was the job, right? You found him. The job's over. Get paid and move on."

"Yeah," I said, "yeah, you may be right. Still..." I tapped my finger on his counter. "Thanks for the call, Gibson."

"Sure thing, glad to help. Say, were you ever a cop?"

"For a short time, yeah."

"Here in New York?"

I nodded, then asked him a question to head him off

before he asked the obvious one.

"Does this job suit you after all the years wearing a badge?"

"Oh, this is just what I do in my off time," Gibson said, leaning in and lowering his voice. "I'm really a hitman for hire."

I left before he could ask me for more details.

I set up in a doorway across from Burger World to wait. Then I'd follow him, see where he was living now. After that I'd have to figure out whether I was going to talk to him, or just tell his wife where he was.

As far as talking to him, I was real curious about what made him walk out on Monday—apparently for lunch—get a job at Burger World and never come back. I mean, it was his company!

What was going through his head to make him cross the street and apply for a job? And why did they take him? Usually you saw kids working in those places—Burger World, McDonalds, Wendy's, fast food places like that, usually hired kids…didn't they?

My curiosity was going to make me approach and ask him, wasn't it?

CHAPTER SIXTEEN

I decided to take it slow.

Instead of calling Nancy Kessenger and telling her I'd found her husband, I went back to Burger World, got in line and stepped up to Templeton Kessenger's register.

Burger World was the home of the World Burger. On the windows were advertisements for the new Around-the-World Burger, loaded with condiments from different countries around the world.

"Can I help you?" he asked, barely looking at me.

"Yeah, I'll have a World Burger and a drink."

"The World meal?"

"No, just the burger, no fries."

"What size drink?"

"Medium."

"For here or to go?"

"Here."

He punched it in and I paid him.

"Your number's one-oh-three," he said, handing me my receipt.

"Thanks."

"Here's your cup."

I took it, then said, "Kind of old for this job, aren't ya? Seems to me it's mostly kids working here, these days." I looked at the other employees behind the counter. None seemed older than twenty.

"It's a living," he said. "Next?"

"Probably stress free, huh?"

"I guess," Kessenger said. "I've got to help the next customer."

"Sure." I stepped aside to wait for my order.

I watched Kessenger while I waited. He treated everybody the same way. No smile, no eye contact, just got the job done.

When I got my burger and Coke, I took it to a booth by the front window. I watched from there while munching on a burger I really hadn't wanted, and sipped Coke. Kessenger didn't talk much with his co-workers, unless it was to say no mayo or cheese.

I was finishing up, trying to decide what to do next, when a man came out from the back and started cleaning tables. He was a black man in his sixties, wearing a shirt and tie, so I assumed he was the manager, pitching in to help.

"Everything all right, sir?" he asked, as he came to my table.

"Just fine," I said. "I was waited on by that older guy, over there. He was very efficient."

He turned and looked, then said, "That's Temp. He's new here. I guess he's tryin' to make a good impression."

"Well, he did on me."

"Just between you and me, he could be a little friendlier."

"Well, he's certainly older than his co-workers. Maybe he's got nothing to say to them."

"Or them to him," the man said. "I know. I meant, he could be friendlier with the customers."

"Can I ask why you took him on?"

"He needed a job, and he can read," the man said. "He doesn't need the symbols to be on the register keys in order to ring up the orders." He leaned in. "I need to have at least one person I can count on, and I prefer an adult."

"So he just walked in off the street?" I asked.

"Cold turkey, just like that," the manager said. "And I liked him. That doesn't happen a lot. Can I get you anythin' else?"

"No, no," I said. "I'm good. I'm just passing the time."

"Refills are free," the man said. "Don't forget."

"Thanks."

The manager moved on, and I had my answer about how Kessenger got hired. Ally said she caught him staring out the window a lot, looking down at the street. My guess was, he was looking at Burger World, probably wondering what it would be like to work there? So one day he walked out of his office, crossed the street, got a job and didn't go back.

What I couldn't figure out was, why would he pick a place so close to the office? Apparently, he didn't care if anyone saw him. That meant he wasn't hiding, exactly. He figured people from the office didn't go to Burger World, but it had to happen eventually. Somebody would see him, tell his partner, tell his wife...and he didn't care?

I tossed my trash and got half a refill on my Coke. Kessenger was still working the register. I wondered when he went on a break. Maybe I should talk to him, try to figure this out. I could wait for him to go on break or follow him home and do it.

As I watched, the girl working the other register sidled up to Kessenger and said something. He smiled at her, nodded, and said something that made her smile, too. He finished the order he was taking, and then told the next person to go to her register. Business was starting to slow down.

Kessenger went into the back, so I thought maybe he was getting ready to go on break. After fifteen minute I went up to the counter.

"What can get you?" the girl asked.

"How long are your breaks, usually?" I asked.

She stared at me and then said, "Mister, I ain't interested—"

"No, no," I said, "I'm waiting for Mr. Kessenger, and I wanted to know how long his break was."

"Mr. Kess—oh, you mean Temp? He's not on break. He left early."

"I didn't see him leave."

"There's a back door."

"Why would he go out that way?" I asked.

She shrugged. "I dunno what to tell you, Mister. Whataya want with Temp, anyway? Why don't you leave 'im alone? He ain't hurtin' nobody." She was suddenly very defensive of him.

"Where's the manager?"

"In his office."

"And where's that?"

"In the back of the kitch—hey!"

I hopped up on the counter, swiveled on my butt, and got down on the other side. I felt something pull in my thigh, but I didn't let that stop me.

"Hey, you can't—Greg!"

I didn't know who Greg was, but I found out soon. He was apparently the one in the back, making the burgers. He was young, built big, over six feet, but soft.

He looked like a Baby Huey type. (I was showing my age. Who remembered Baby Huey?)

"What is it, Angie—hey, whataya doin' back here?" Greg brandished an empty French fry basket, like he was going to swing it.

"It's okay," I said, holding up my hands, "I'm friends with your manager."

"Oh, okay…" He lowered the basket.

I went past him, dragging the leg I'd hurt crawling over the counter. I hated being fifty! I always think of Molly Shannon on SNL saying, "I'm fifty, and I can kick!" Well, my kicking days were over, obviously, if I couldn't even climb over a fast food counter without getting a charley horse.

CHAPTER SEVETEEN

"He ain't friends with the manager!" I heard the girl telling him.

"Well, he said he was."

"You gotta throw him out."

"I ain't a bouncer," he complained.

"Oh, you're such a baby!"

I kept going back until I saw an open door, and part of a desk. As I entered the manager I had talked to earlier looked up from his desk, obviously expecting to see one of his employees.

"What are you doing back here?" he demanded. "You're not allowed—"

"It's okay," I said, "we talked out front, remember."

"Yes, I do remember," the man said, "but you still can't come back—"

"Did you tell Temp Kessenger I was asking about him?" I asked, cutting him off. "Is that why he left early?"

"Well, yes, I did tell him," he said. "And he asked for the rest if the day off."

"And went out the back."

"Yes."

"Why did you tell him?"

"Look, I know he's runnin' from something," the man

said. "I thought he should know a policeman was asking about him."

"A polic—I'm not a policeman. What made you think that?"

"Well...you were asking questions...if you're not a policeman, then who are you?"

I gave him my card.

"A private eye?" he asked. "Really?" He was looking at me askance. (Webster says "askance" means someone is looking at you "with disapproval or mistrust." I knew that word because, as I got older, more and more people seemed to be looking at me that way.)

"That's right," I said.

He handed it back.

"Who hired you?" he asked.

"His wife, she's worried about him. He's been missing for a few days."

"A few days?"

"Isn't that when he started working here?"

"Well, yes—"

"Apparently he left his wife, a large house and a lucrative job to work here."

"That's odd. Why would he do that?"

"Exactly what I was going to ask him, before you warned him off."

"But...aren't you supposed to tell his wife where he is?"

"I am, but I thought we'd talk, first. She's not really my idea of a warm, loving wife."

"Tell me about it," he said. "Oh, not that I know her, but I had one of those. Geez, now I'm kinda glad I'm helpin' him."

"Well, you could help him more by telling me where

he's living."

He looked dismayed.

"Oh, I don't think I can do that," he said. "I mean, whatever he is, he's still an employee."

Damn. A conscientious manager.

"All right, then," I said, handing him my card again. "Take this back. Give him my number. Tell him if I don't hear from him by tomorrow night, I'll call his wife and tell her where he is."

"All right."

"What's your name?"

"Frank Woodley."

"Thank you, Mr. Woodley," I said.

"You're welcome, Mr..." he looked at the card. "...Headstone."

I just nodded and walked out.

CHAPTER EIGHTEEN

I knew my responsibility was to my client, but I felt the need to talk to Kessenger first. And I had just given him about twenty-four hours to do that. Which left me free to serve some papers for that lawyer friend of mine who still threw me some work. And because he sent work my way, I served his papers for free.

I found his message on my phone after leaving Burger World and told him I'd pick the papers up at his office first thing the next morning, so that's what I did.

"My morning, Headstone," he reminded me, deliberately mispronouncing my name, "not yours."

See, I don't mind when my friends call me that.

After serving the papers I had thought about waiting for the girl from the Burger World register to leave work and ask her where Kessenger lived, but she might think I was stalking her. After all, as far as she was concerned, I'd already tried to pick her up twice.

I went back to my office instead, hoping that Kessenger would call either my landline or my cell. I caught up on some paperwork, typing my report on the Kessenger case, as far as it had gone. By the time I was finished, I was hungry.

* * *

As I rode the old elevator down, I could feel how empty the building was, since it was after working hours. A lot of the building had been renovated, minus my office, and the old elevators. They moved so slowly that you could imagine you were back in history, and when you got out it would be the early twentieth-century again. Sometimes I didn't think that would be such a bad thing.

When I did get out it was still 2017, so I left the building, with intentions of getting something to eat and going home.

"Hey, P.I.!" somebody yelled.

I turned and saw tattooed Ally from Herman James rushing toward me.

"What are you doing here?" I asked.

"I looked you up, Headstone," she said. "In the phone book. I wanted to see where you work."

"The building's empty now, my office is closed," I said. "And the elevator ride is too slow to go back up."

"Oh, I've been up there, already," she said. "You weren't around, so I let myself in. I saw where my desk will be."

"Your desk?"

"Sure, when you hire me. You've got lots of desks. I picked one out."

"Ally—"

"You had that many people workin' for you at one time?" she asked.

"I did."

"Geez, somethin' bad musta happened."

"What about your job at Herman James?"

"They didn't waste any time," she said. "They let me

go today. Did you find Mr. Kessenger?"

Since I hadn't told his wife yet that I'd found him, I didn't feel I could confide that information to Ally. After all, she didn't work for me.

"Not yet," I said.

"Well, I guess if you do they can rehire me," she said, "or hire somebody else to work for him. Maybe by then I'll be working for you."

"Now we never agreed—"

"Where are you headed?"

"Home."

"You ain't workin' tonight?"

"I do have down time, Ally," I said. "Tonight I'll be home, reading a book or watching TV."

"That's not what the private eyes on TV do," she pointed out.

"I'm not a TV private eye."

"No, I guess not."

"Why don't you go home, Ally," I suggested. "There's nothing to be done tonight."

"Here." She handed me a piece of paper.

"What's this?"

"My phone number," she said. "You're gonna need me before this is over, P.I. Gimme a call. G'night."

She started trotting away the way she had come and I suddenly came up with one outstanding question I wanted to ask her.

"Hey!"

"Yeah?" She turned.

"How did you get into my office?"

She smiled at me.

"I got lots of hidden talents, P.I.," she said. "You'll find out."

I watched as she ran up Fifth Avenue and then disappeared around the corner. After looking at the phone number on the slip of paper—it was obviously a cell number, with no New York area code—I stuck it in my pocket. It never really occurred to me that I'd be fishing it back out soon because she'd be right. I'd need her.

CHAPTER NINETEEN

My kitchen was usually pretty spotless. I didn't always eat my take-out there, and the only thing I ever prepared for myself was coffee. I had a Mr. Coffee, and usually made ten cups and then microwaved it over the next few days cup-by-cup. I probably should've bought a single cup coffee maker, but old habits die as hard as they say.

I was microwaving a cup of coffee that night after finishing my take-out Chinese dinner when my cell phone started to vibrate on the kitchen counter. I waited for the last beep of the microwave before answering it. The incoming phone number was unfamiliar to me.

"Hello?"

"Is this Mr., uh, Headstone?"

"That's right."

"This is Templeton Kessenger."

"Mr. Kessenger," I said, "I'm so glad you called—"

"Frank Woodley, the manager at Burger World, gave me your number."

"Yes, I asked him to do that."

"Can I ask why?"

"Because we need to talk, Mr. Kessenger," I said, "before I tell your wife what I've found out."

"You mean, about me working at Burger World?"

"Yes."

"Why haven't you told her, yet?"

"I'm not sure, to tell you the truth," I said. "I just thought there was more to the story."

"What story?"

"That you just...disappeared. Didn't come home."

He was quiet.

"Mr. Kessenger?"

"I have to work tomorrow," he said. "I told Woodley I'd be in. Can you come there? We can talk on my break."

"Burger World?"

"That's where I work."

"That's one of the things I want to talk to you about."

"Tomorrow," he said, and hung up.

I spent the next morning serving papers for my lawyer friend, Steve Ryder, then went to the Burger World on Wall Street (sounds funny even now) to see Kessenger.

As I entered, he was working behind his register. It had been a while since I'd had Burger World, and now I got in line to get it for the third time in two days, from him.

When it was my turn, he looked at me and said, "Mr. Headston."

"That's right." And it was!

"Thank you for coming. I'll be going on break in fifteen minutes. Would you like something?"

"I'll just take a World meal," I said.

"Comin' up." He charged me for it. I waited, and when he called my number, I picked it up and managed to get a booth by the front window. I had taken a few bites when he came over carrying a drink and sat across from me.

"I can see your window from here," I said, "across the street."

"I know," he said. He was a handsome man in his late forties, who looked fairly ridiculous in his Burger World outfit. "I spent a lot of time standing at that window, looking down here, imagining what a stress-free job this must be."

"So that was your motive for disappearing and getting the job here?"

"I didn't disappear," he said. "I'm right here, across the street from my old office. I just haven't gone back home."

"And you have a new place to live?"

"Yes, I took an apartment in Tribeca."

Tribeca was a trendy section of downtown that would afford him easy access to Wall Street.

"But why stay on Wall Street?" I asked. "Why not get a job in a Burger World somewhere else?"

"I told you," he said. "I'm not hiding."

"But you know that no one from your office comes to Burger World."

He shrugged.

"What if they did, and they saw you?"

He shrugged again.

"Mr. Kessenger, is there some reason I shouldn't tell your wife, or your partner, where you are?"

"Probably not," he said. "I knew I'd have to talk to them eventually."

"What about your share of the company?"

"That's what I was going to have to talk to them about," he said. "How to split my part up."

"What were your intentions?" I asked. "To sign it over to your wife? Or let your partner buy you out?"

"I hadn't decided, yet," he said. "After all, I only walked out and got this job a few days ago."

"So you were waiting to see if you liked it here? And the stress-free life it offered?"

"I suppose," he said. "I didn't want to make any rash decisions."

"This wasn't a rash decision?"

"Oh, no," he said. "I told you, I stood at that window every day for a long time, looking down here."

"That was what your girl, Ally, told me."

"She's a good kid," he said. "Did they fire her?"

"They let her go."

"Damn," he said. "I was hoping they'd just give her to another executive."

"Well, they didn't. She was a consequence of your decision. And there will probably be others."

"I know," he said. "I'll make it up to her."

"How? Give her part of the company?"

He laughed at that.

"Look, Mr. Headston, I never intended for my decision to harm the company."

"Or your wife?"

"My leaving my wife would not harm her in the least."

"But leaving your company would harm it. I've been told you're the reason it's a success."

"Scott will be able to keep it going," he said. "He's got some young go-getters on the staff."

I looked out the window at the people walking by. One or two turned their heads and looked inside. I wondered when someone from Herman James would have looked in and spotted Kessenger behind the register? Or maybe one of them would have had a sudden urge for onion rings.

I finished my food and pushed the tray aside. We both held our cups.

"Well," I said, "you haven't given me a reason not to notify your wife."

"She's your client," he said. "I understand."

"I don't suppose you'd like to give me your new address so I can pass it on to her?"

"Well," he said, "I don't want to make things too easy for her."

"Fine," I said. "I'll just tell her I found you working in a Burger World across the street from the Herman James building."

"That'll blow her mind," he said, with a grin. "What about Scott?"

"He's not my client," I pointed out. "I'll let her tell him."

"And she will," he said, shaking his head. "He won't believe it."

"So the stress," I said, "it came from...what? Your marriage? Your job?"

"All of it," he said. "My *life*. I was getting too depressed about it."

"Did you see a psychiatrist?"

"Oh, yes," he said, "I've been in therapy for two years. Nobody knows about that, either. But it didn't help. I knew the only thing that would help was a change." He gestured with his hand. "This."

"This?"

"For now," he said. "Mr. Woodley was nice enough to hire me off the street. It surprised me, but I thought it was also an indication that I had made the right decision." He looked at his watch. "I have to get back. I don't want to get fired." He extended his hand and I shook it. "Thank you for giving me a chance to explain. Now you can make Nancy understand it."

"Believe me," I said, as he got up, "I'm going to try."

I thought about going to Westchester County to tell Mrs. Kessenger about her husband, but it was a long trip. I decided to go to my office, write out my report, call her and tell her about it, and then mail it to her with my bill. I figured that ought to put "the end" on this case.

Yeah, right!

CHAPTER TWENTY

"He works where?"

"Burger World."

Her tone was incredulous.

"Is he crazy?"

"He seemed pretty sane to me."

"You spoke with him?"

"Yes."

"Did he say why he did it?"

"To relieve the stress in his life," I said. "Any more than that you'll have to get from him."

"Do you know where he's living?"

"Somewhere in Tribeca," I said. "He wouldn't give me the address."

"Couldn't you have followed him home?"

"I could have—"

"I'd like you to do that, Mr. Headstone," she said, still getting my name wrong—but she was paying for that privilege. "Please follow him home, and then give me the address of where he lives, and the...the Burger World." She made them sound like the two dirtiest words in history.

"I'll pay you well," she added.

"Don't worry, Mrs. Kessenger," I said, "I'll take care

of it—and you'll get my bill at my usual rate."

"Thank you…John? May I call you that?"

"Sure," I said.

At least she'd stop calling me "Headstone."

I had mixed feelings about following Kessenger home from Burger World. But it was Nancy Kessenger who was my client, so later that day I was standing across the street, in a doorway, waiting for him to come out. When he did, I fell in behind him, followed him all the way home.

It was a short subway ride to Chambers Street, but eventually I watched him go into a warehouse building which had been renovated into apartments. This was not the kind of neighborhood Robert DeNiro and Beyoncé lived in, but the rents would have still been considerable.

DeNiro co-founded the Tribeca Film Festival, which was supposed to—and did—revitalize the area following the 9/11 attack. The actor also had a restaurant on Greenwich Street called The Tribeca Grill, co-owned by the Myriad Group, which also owned the famous Nobu Restaurant.

I didn't spend a lot of time in Tribeca, which bordered Soho, another part of the city I didn't spend much time in. Not my scene, as we used to say when we were kids. I'm a lover of old New York, so gentrified neighborhoods are not my favorite thing—not in Manhattan, and certainly not in Brooklyn. Give me old Sheepshead Bay, any day.

But here I was in Tribeca, watching Templeton Kessenger enter his new home. He may have been looking to reduce stress in his life, but he was still a wealthy man with certain tastes and living well was one of them.

Once he had gone inside, I approached the building to locate the exact address somewhere on the side of it. I also tried to enter, but found it locked. Nancy Kessenger was going to have to settle for the street location, and not the apartment number or floor.

As I started down the steps, I heard the front door open behind me and a woman came out. I tried to dart back up the stairs to get inside before the door closed, but she wasn't having it.

She blocked the way with her stocky body and said, "Whoa. Private building, bub."

I watched the door close and latch behind her.

"I just wanted to find out if there were any vacancies," I lied.

She was dressed well, but not a clothes horse, being kind of lumpy as she approached fifty.

"Nope," she said, "you're outta luck. Fella just took the last one last week."

That would've been Kessenger.

"So no available apartments?"

"No apartments, at all," she said. "You've got to take half a floor. This fella took the fourth—the top floor."

"Wow, that must've been expensive," I said.

"They're all the same price," she said, "and yeah, expensive."

She moved around me and went the rest of the way down the stairs.

"Well, thanks for the information," I said. "Have a nice day."

She waved a hand without turning back to look at me as she walked down the street.

I went back up the stairs to look through the glass on

the door. There were four rows of mailboxes. They all looked like they had name tags—which I couldn't read from my vantage point—except one. The boxes were in line according to floor, that would've been the fourth.

Since I'd gotten as much as I was going to get—which was probably enough—I went back down the stone steps and headed off in the lumpy lady's wake.

I went back to the office, got on my computer and emailed Nancy Kessenger my final report, and bill. Sending bills out that way was something I was playing with.

Three days later the check arrived, paying my bill in full. Sending it by email worked. It was paid promptly.

Four days after that, Templeton Kessenger was dead.

CHAPTER TWENTY-ONE

I had spent the four days serving papers, taking photographs for an insurance company, and following a wayward husband who turned out not to be cheating on his wife, but on his diet.

I was writing up a report when I heard the outer door of my office open. Footsteps approached my door, which was open, and two men wearing suits entered.

Cops.

"John Headstone?" the older one asked.

"Headstone is the name of the agency," I told him. "My name is John Headston."

"Right." He took out his wallet, flipped it open for me to see his NYPD ID and detective shield. "I'm Detective Leon, this is my partner, Detective Stokes."

Leon was in his forties, starting to show thickness around his middle and grey at his temples. Stokes was black, in his thirties, and at this time in his career, took in everything around him.

"Where's the rest of your staff?" he asked. "That's a lot of empty desks out there."

"They're on vacation."

"All of them?"

"It's a group trip," I said. "Can I help you?"

"Yes," Leon said, "we want to ask you about a man named Templeton Kessenger. Do you know him."

"I know who he is, yes."

"How?"

"His wife hired me to find him."

"He was missing?"

"Yes," I said. "Is he missing again? Is that why you're here? Why you and not White Plains? Or are they still not interested?"

"They weren't interested when he went missing?"

"No," I said, "they blew his wife off, and then blew me off."

He paused to take something out of his pocket, unwrap it and stick it in his mouth. I couldn't tell if it was a lozenge, a cough drop, or he just liked candy. At least it wasn't a Kojak lollipop.

"Who'd you talk to there?"

I dredged up the name of the cop I talked to and gave it to him. Stokes wrote it down.

"So you found the hubby?" Leon asked.

"Yes, he was working in a Burger World across from his old job and living in a place in Tribeca. I gave his wife all the details."

"Burger World?" Leon said. "He left a high-priced job to work in Burger World?"

"That's right."

"Did he say why?"

"To cut down on the stress in his life."

"And did he leave his wife for the same reason?" They hadn't sat down and I hadn't stood up. Now I leaned back so that my chair creaked.

"Apparently," I said. "Look, what's this about? Are you guys missing persons, or what?"

"Or what," Stokes said.

"We're homicide," Leon said.

"Homicide?" I said. "Who's dead?"

"Kessenger."

I came forward in my chair.

"How? When?"

They exchanged a glance, probably signaling each other as to whether or not they believed my ignorance.

"He was found yesterday morning," Leon said. "In his apartment."

"By who?"

"A cleaning lady."

"How was he killed?"

"Bludgeoned," Leon said, "apparently in his sleep."

"Somebody beat him to death while he was sleeping, and he didn't wake up and fight?"

"Apparently not," Stokes said. "The first blow must've killed him, the M.E. said."

"He must've been a heavy sleeper," Leon said.

"Have you talked to his wife?"

"Oh yes," Leon said. "We've done our job, Mr. Headston. We saw her yesterday. Made the notification and questioned her at the same time."

"Does she have an alibi?"

"Do you have an alibi, Headston?" Leon asked. It didn't escape my notice that he got my name right twice in a row.

I was shocked by the question. Why suspect me? What had Nancy Kessenger told them?

"For when?"

"Let's see...that would be Tuesday night, between midnight and, let's say, four."

"What are most people doing at that time of night?"

I asked. "I was home in bed."

"Alone?" Stokes asked.

"Yes, alone."

"Can you prove it?" Leon asked.

"No."

"No neighbor who can corroborate your story?"

"It's not a story," I said. "I was asleep. Why do I need an alibi, anyway? I did my job."

"Did you talk to him while you were doing your job?"

"Yes, I did."

"Isn't that unusual with wayward husband work?" Leon asked.

"He interested me," I said. "A Wall Street hustler who gave it up one afternoon, just like that. Cold turkey."

"So you asked him why?" Leon asked.

"I gave him a chance to convince me not to tell his wife I'd found him."

"And?"

"He didn't. He told me to go ahead and tell her, so I did."

"What did she say?"

"I told her where he worked, but she wanted to know where he lived, too. So I spent another half-a-day getting her that information."

"Did you talk to him again?"

"No."

They exchanged another glance, I guessed they were trying to decide if we were done.

"Have you talked to his partner?" I asked.

"Like I said," Leon answered, digging into his pocket again. "We did our job." He unwrapped and put it in his mouth, and pocketed the wrapper. "Okay, Headston, thanks. We'll be in touch."

"Don't leave town," Stokes said.

"Am I a suspect?"

"Your name came up," Leon said. "That's all. Just routine."

"Wow."

"What?"

"I thought they only said that on *Blue Bloods*."

Leon grinned. "I like that show," he said, and they left.

CHAPTER TWENTY-TWO

I sat and brooded a while.

They couldn't have really considered me a suspect. I had absolutely no motive. But they could label me a "person of interest," and haul me in at some future time for more questioning.

I couldn't believe Kessenger was dead—murdered in his sleep. How many people were aware of his new address, I wondered? He probably gave it to his job, and I had given it to his wife. One of those two must have passed it to someone else.

I didn't know if the cops were working on that premise. I also couldn't work on an active police investigation without risking my license. But if I had something to do with Temple Kessenger getting killed, it didn't sit right with me.

It was my guess that the number one suspect was Nancy Kessenger. It was also my guess that she had engaged the services of a lawyer. What I needed to do was get that lawyer to engage my services. If I was working for him, then the cops couldn't take my license away, even if I got in their way.

Despite the fact that my once twelve-man staff was down to one, that I had become a glorified process server at fifty years old, and that my career was going nowhere, I was good at what I did—or what I used to do. I was a good investigator at one time, and it was my belief that I still was.

I picked up my cell and called Nancy Kessenger's number.

Nancy Kessenger agreed to see me at her house and have her attorney there. I Lyfted my way there from the train station and rang the doorbell with five minutes to spare, at 11:55 a.m.

She answered the door and invited me in. I followed her tight backside to the living room, watching it twitch inside a short skirt. The high heels had something to do with it, but I flattered myself that it was also for my benefit.

A man in an expensive, grey, three-piece suit stood up from the sofa, setting a coffee cup down on the table in front of him.

"Mr. Headstone is it?" he asked, extending his hand.

"Headston," I said, taking his hand and shaking it, "John Headston, of the Headstone Agency."

"Ah," he said, "my name is Seymour Griffith, Griffith, Wymouth and Estevez."

"Estevez?" I repeated.

He grinned. "Estevez."

"Would you like a cup of coffee, Mr. Headston?" she asked.

"Yes, please."

"I'll get it."

Griffith watched her ass as she walked out, then saw me watching him watching her. He grinned boyishly, if a man in his forties with grey hair can do that—and he could.

"She's a fine woman," he said.

"Is she in trouble?" I asked.

"She's the wife of a murdered man," he said.

"Right," I said, "the number one suspect."

"My firm has investigators, Mr. Headston," he said. "Good ones. Why should we hire you?"

"I have a head start," I said. "I knew the man."

"You spoke with him when you found him?"

"Yes."

"What did he tell you?"

"That he was looking to relieve his stress."

"By leaving home? And a high paying job?" he asked. "For Burger World?"

"Exactly."

"That doesn't sound right," he said. "It sounds way too extreme for there not to have been something else going on with him."

"I agree," I told him. "And that's why I think I can help. I've been up to the Herman James offices. They know me there. Your guy is going to have to start over, and they may clam up on him."

"And what does this have to do with my client, Mrs. Kessenger?"

"The detectives will be operating under the assumption that she's a suspect," I explained, "and not only that, but the number one suspect."

"And you will not?"

"I will not," I confirmed. "If I'm working for you, then your client is my client. I'll look for the guilty parties elsewhere."

The lawyer gave the matter due consideration before

speaking again.

"You think you can solve Kessenger's murder before the police do?"

"I think I can find proof that Mrs. Kessenger didn't kill her husband," I lied. After all, I really wasn't convinced that she hadn't done it, or had it done. "That's not something they're even going to be looking for."

Nancy Kessenger came back into the room and handed me a cup of coffee.

"Did I miss anything?" she asked, looking at us both with her penciled eyebrows raised.

"You're hired, Mr. Headston," Griffith said.

CHAPTER TWENTY-THREE

I felt guilty—just a little.

I had lied to Nancy Kessenger's lawyer in order to get him to hire me (he paid me five dollars). He didn't have a single on him.) It was all I needed to have the protection of his client attorney/client privilege). I made him think I was completely confident that Nancy Kessenger had nothing to do with her husband's death, when that wasn't the case, at all. I knew, just as well as the police did, that the wife was the number one suspect.

But in one way I hadn't lied to him. I was going to try my best to find out who really killed Temple Kessenger, so I very well might end up clearing his client of any suspicion.

I wanted to question Nancy Kessenger, but not in front of her lawyer, so I told them both I'd be in touch, and left after arranging for Griffith to have his secretary email me a letter stating I was now in his employ regarding Nancy Kessenger.

I used my cell to call for my Lyft to the train station, and then during the ride back to Manhattan thought about Templeton Kessenger. I had spent very little time with the guy, but I'd liked him. And if I had anything to do with fingering him for his killer, I wanted to find out.

Back in Manhattan I returned to my office, found the letter I wanted on Griffith, Wymouth and Estevez letterhead in my email and printed it out.

With the letter in my pocket I left the office and set off to start my first murder investigation in over fifteen years.

When I had come back from a two-year suspension of my license and returned to my office, it was empty. My twelve-man staff had moved on to other positions, because they all had to make a living. And so did I. I tried for a few years to resurrect my career, but over the course of a few years it had become clear that law firms were not going to employ me, not for important investigations like murder. So I ended up plying my trade as a glorified process server.

But now I was involved in a real case.

Detective Leon and Stokes were working out of Manhattan South Homicide, which was headquartered in the One Police Plaza building. I identified myself at the desk in the lobby, and they called upstairs and received permission to send me up. When the elevator doors opened, Detective Stokes was standing there. He was jacketless, with his white shirt sleeves rolled up.

"This way," he said.

I followed.

"How did you know we wanted to talk to you?" he asked, looking over his shoulder.

"I didn't," I said. "I came here to talk to you guys."

"About what?"

"Probably the same thing you want to talk to me about."

"Well," he said, "that's convenient."

He led me to a doorway that led to a bullpen filled with detective desks, only about half of them occupied. One of the occupants was Detective Leon, also in shirt sleeves.

"Mr. Headstone," Leon said, "so good of you to come in."

"He didn't know we were looking for him," Stokes said, sitting across from his partner at his own desk. "He came in to talk to us."

"Well," Leon said, "pull up a chair and we'll talk."

I snagged a visitor's chair and sat so I could look at both of them.

"Why don't we go first?" Leon suggested. "I mean, since you're in our office."

"Sure, go ahead."

They had more questions about Templeton Kessenger, like what I'd seen while watching him, and what we'd talked about. They made me go over it several times, just in case I knew something I didn't know I knew. It was a tried and true technique, designed to bring out information. Unfortunately, it didn't help them very much. I had pretty much told them everything I knew about Kessenger the first time they'd questioned me.

"Okay," Leon said, "before we get to why you're here, can we get you anything? Water? Soft drink? Coffee?"

"No, I'm fine," I said, "but thanks for asking. Is this Manhattan South's version of hospitality?"

"You haven't tasted our coffee," Stokes said.

"Maybe next time," I said.

"So what's on your mind, Mr. Headstone?" Leon asked.

"I'd like to get a look inside Temple Kessenger's residence. Since it's a crime scene, I knew I'd need your permission."

"I appreciate that," Leon said. "You could have just broken in."

"And risk my license? Not likely."

"That's right," Leon said. "I understand you've had previous problems regarding your license."

So they had checked me out, and pretty thoroughly, too. That wasn't unexpected.

"Well, this time I intend to hang onto it," I said.

"And why do you want to get inside his place?" Stokes asked. "You wouldn't be working on an active police investigation, would you?"

"Not a chance," I said. I leaned over and handed Leon the letter from Nancy Kessenger's lawyer. He read it, then handed it across to his partner.

"Odd that this law firm would hire you when I'm sure they have their own investigators," Leon said.

"It was Griffith," I told them. "And it was Nancy Kessenger's idea. Apparently, they want to keep her very happy."

"Doesn't Mrs. Kessenger trust us to solve her husband's murder?" Leon asked.

"I'm sure she does," I said, "as long as you don't try to pin it on her."

"Now we wouldn't do a thing like that," Stokes said, handing the letter back to me.

"Unless, of course," Leon added, "she did it."

CHAPTER TWENTY-FOUR

When I got to Temple Kessenger's building I had to get myself up to the fourth floor. Luckily, somebody was coming out the front door as I got there. It was the same yhick-bodied lady who had blocked me the last time I was there, but I was quicker this time. I did an end run around her and caught the door before it closed.

"Hey!" she protested.

"Relax," I said, "I'm going up to four to see the cop there."

As the door closed, I heard her shout, "Well, why didn't ya tell me you were a cop?"

I'd never do that!

Upstairs I saw the cop sitting in a chair in front of the door to Kessenger's place.

"Sorry, sir," he said, standing when he saw me. He put his hand out like he was stopping traffic. "Nobody's allowed in there."

"Officer Sterling," I said, reading his name plate, "my name's Headston. I've got permission from Detective Leon to go in and have a look around. I'm working the case for an attorney."

"I wasn't told—"

"Here you go," I said, handing him Leon's card,

which the detective had given to me as I left. "There's a note on the back."

The young cop looked at the front of the card first, then turned it over.

"It says you can go in," he said, "but how do I know you didn't write this?"

"You've got the card, with the detective's phone number," I said. "I suggest you call him, if you have doubts. But when I was on the job—admittedly a long time ago—I always tried to use my own initiative. The higher-ups like that."

"You were on the job?"

"For a while," I said, "before I went private. But I was working Brooklyn South back then."

"Still the job," Sterling said. "I guess it's okay."

He stood aside, and then even opened the door for me. "Thanks."

He handed me Leon's card as I went in, and I put it back in my pocket. It was legit, although I had taken one of his business cards off his desk, in case I needed it later. I have to admit, there was a time when I wasn't afraid to bend the rules. That was when I was young and full of piss and vinegar. Now I'm older and the thought of it makes me piss myself—almost.

Inside I saw that it was a loft, covering the entire length of the building. But for the most part it was bare. There were large expanses of empty floor. Only in one corner of the loft was there any furniture—a bed, a chest of drawers, a table and two chairs, and a sofa. Against the wall was a stove, and a sink. The only other thing I could see was, in another corner, a bathroom set-up, with a sink, commode and tub.

The loft must have been eighteen hundred square feet,

but the living space seemed not more than four hundred. This was a sparse way for anyone to live, let alone a man with Kessenger's money. Was he punishing himself, somehow? Forcing himself to live well below his means? Except that the rent here must've been sky high. Why spend a ton on rent, and not furnish the place? Perhaps he didn't mean to stay long.

I went through the chest of drawers, found new clothing—socks underwear, T-shirts, folded button-down shirts. I looked around, saw something I hadn't seen before—a closet. It seemed to be the only one. I opened the door, found a windbreaker, and a sports jacket on hangers, and that was it. If he stayed longer in a couple of months, he'd have had to buy a heavier coat.

I looked under the bed, found nothing. I didn't expect to. The cops had gone through the place. Anything obvious they would have found.

I walked across the floor to the bathroom set-up. The sink was bare, not part of a cabinet-and-counter set up. The only surface for anything was the top of the toilet tank. There I saw a cup with a toothbrush in it, a comb and an electric razor. I looked around, found one electrical outlet for the razor.

I looked at the bathtub next. Kessenger hadn't lived there long enough for there to be anything like mold or a ring. I took a pen from my pocket and poked down into the drain. Nothing.

I went back to the furniture. The sofa looked like good quality, the wide, three cushion kind. I picked up all the cushions to have a look underneath. Nothing.

I stood in the center of the eighteen hundred square feet, hoping something that the cops missed would catch my eye. Detective Leon had been willing to let me come up here but hadn't said a word about whether or not they had found something. I was thinking he was laughing his head off, because there was nothing here to find. In fact, there was almost nothing up here, at all. Just a big, almost empty space that certainly did not feel lived in.

I left, thanking Officer Sterling for letting me in. Outside, on the steps, I ran into the thick-bodied woman again, this time coming in.

"We've gotta stop meeting like this," she said, with a smile. I supposed now that she knew I wasn't a peeper or burglar, I was worth a smile. It certainly changed her face into something a lot more appealing.

"You just come down from upstairs?" she asked.

"Yes."

"That fella, he didn't talk to anybody in the building a lot," she said.

"I didn't think—"

"Except me." She looked proud.

"You and he spoke?"

She nodded. "Several times."

"About what?"

She closed one eye, stared at me and asked, "You like tea?"

CHAPTER TWENTY-FIVE

Her name was Elizabeth Munnings. She told me to call her Beth, not Betty.

"All I ever think of when I hear Betty is Betty Boop or Betty and Veronica," she said, "and I don't look like either of them."

She didn't look like them, for sure. I figured her for mid- or late-forties, about five-foot-five, with short dark hair that was shot with grey, and a pug nose that might've been cute twenty years ago. She did, however, seem to have nice skin, and pretty blue eyes.

She let us into her apartment with a key.

"I know," she said, "It don't look like much, but it's mine. I moved here after my divorce eight years ago. The rent's high, but I did all right in my settlement."

"Good for you."

"Have a seat," she said. "I'll make some tea, unless—" she turned to give me a suggestive look, "—you'd like something stronger?"

"A little early in the day, for me," I admitted.

"Yeah, you're right," she said. "Be right back."

She had matching furniture that seemed to be good quality. The apartment was clean, too, no dust that I could see on any surface. There was a fifty-inch TV on a stand just large enough to hold it, and next to it was a packed DVD tower. I went over to have a look at what she'd been watching. In among the blockbuster movies like *Avatar* and *Star Wars* were a few with titles suggesting they were X-rated. I was back on the sofa when she came in carrying the tea on a tray with some cookies.

"There," she said, sitting next to me on the sofa and setting the tray down on a clear, glass coffee table.

"Thank you, Beth."

"Sugar?"

"No, just the way it is."

She handed me my tea cup, then picked up her own.

"Can we get back to you and Temple Kessenger?"

"Was that his name?"

"You didn't know his name?"

"Well," she said, "you'll notice it wasn't on the mailbox downstairs."

I did notice that.

"And he just introduced himself as Temp." She shrugged. "That's how I knew him."

"What did you two talk about?"

"Not much," she said. "Just shot the breeze, discussed the weather, the high rent, the garbage pick-up."

Somehow, without me noticing, she'd managed to move closer to me on the sofa. Also, that close I detected the fragrance of some freshly applied perfume. It had been a long time since I'd experienced the seductive talents of a woman. After all, I was now middle-aged with a middle spread, and did not have much of a love life, at all. In fact, it had been quite some time for me, so I thought I was probably imagining things.

Until she kissed me.

It was accomplished with a lunge, and suddenly her

mouth was on mine, and her tongue was in my mouth. After the initial shock I realized it was not all that unpleasant, and I started to lean into it.

Then she pulled away.

"I'm sorry," she said, "I just thought—well, this is the third time you've run into me on the stairs. I thought, maybe, it was...intentional?"

Her eyes had a hopeful look in them, and her hand had found its way to my thigh. Although neither of us was in our prime, the situation itself was so charged with sexual tension that my body had no choice but to react. When she moved her hand further up my thigh she came into contact with the result.

"Oh, my..." she said, took my hand and led me to the bedroom.

CHAPTER TWENTY-SIX

As I said, it had been a long time.

I fumbled a bit, at first, but finally we were naked and in her bed. As I'd suspected, her skin was very smooth and she was soft all over. While she had a bit of a spare tire, her breasts and butt were nicely cushioned and curved. She was the kind of woman you wouldn't imagine doing this with, but now, in the midst of it all, it was nothing but pleasurable.

She had dark, large nipples which she allowed me to concentrate on for a while, but then she became impatient. She went down on me to get me good and slick, and then mounted me. As I said, it had been a while...

"Sorry," I said, moments later. "That was quick. I'm a little out of practice."

"Really? A policeman like you? I'd think you did this all the time with—what do you call them—suspects?"

"You're not a suspect," I said, "you're—well, if anything, a witness."

"Well," she said, "I really didn't witness anything."

We were lying side-by-side, so I turned my head to look at her. With the passion spent, and the lamp next to the bed on, I could see her double chin and the lines in her face. Also her body, which had looked robust while we were actually fucking, now looked saggy. They say even bad sex is good sex, and maybe that's true, but in the aftermath—not afterglow—of this coupling, I felt sad.

I sat up and reached for my clothes.

"What do you mean?" I asked.

"Well...I really didn't know the guy all that well," she said. "I sort of...fudged the story a bit to get you into my apartment."

I stood up and buckled my pants.

"You mean you lied to have sex?"

"Well, yeah," she said, propping herself up on one elbow. Her hair was a matted mess, her make-up smeared. It wasn't a pretty sight. "I mean, I like sex, and I can't be picky about it."

I grabbed my shirt, feeling stupid and duped. And yeah, used.

"What's that look?" she asked. "Okay, I know I ain't great, but hell, you're no prize. We fucked. So what? What'd you expect?"

"I don't know what I expected," I said. "I don't know what I'm doing here." Luckily my shoes were loafers, so I just slipped into them. "I'm out of here."

I headed out the bedroom door, but halfway across the living room to the front door I heard her shout, "Lemme know if you wanna go again, some time."

And she laughed, a cackle that followed me down the stairs and out into the street.

I walked for a while, instead of hailing a cab or calling Lyft. I felt foolish and sad. Was my life so empty that I grabbed at the first free fuck that came along, no matter who it was? On the other hand, she was right, I was no prize. But I was wishing I had left her apartment two seconds after I ejaculated. Then maybe I wouldn't be feeling so empty.

I came to a diner and stopped in for a cup of coffee. It was an old-time place, with a pedestal on the counter with some pie in it.

"I'll have a piece of that," I said to the guy behind the counter.

"It's been there all day," he warned.

It was only early evening, so that had to be a matter of hours.

Then I realized I was hungry.

"What's your special tonight?"

"Same as every night," he said. "Meatloaf."

"I'll take it."

He refilled my coffee while I waited, and then set the plate down on front of me, steaming with meatloaf and mashed potatoes, all covered with brown gravy. I took a bite. It was good.

"Whataya so down about?" he asked. "Look at me? You're my dinner rush, and I ain't so down."

"I just had sex."

"Jeez," he said, "it's been a long time for me. Tell me about it." He leaned on the counter, an overweight, middle-aged man looking for some vicarious thrills. His eyes were wide while he waited for the details.

"She wasn't much," I said, "but then, like she pointed out, neither am I."

"Man," he said, "I get so horny, sometimes I'd fuck a hole in the ground. I envy ya, pal. Hey, I'll be back for more details."

A couple came in and he went to serve them.
He envied me.
Maybe I wasn't such a sad sack, after all.
I ate my meatloaf, feeling a little lighter.

CHAPTER TWENTY-SEVEN

I didn't have time to get to Herman James before they closed down for the day. I'd have to save that for tomorrow. But I did have time to get to the Wall Street Burger World. I walked in, not tempted at all after my meatloaf.

The same girl was working the counter, so I waited in line.

"Whataya have?" she asked.

"Is the manager here?" I asked. "Mr. Woodley?"

"He's in his off—hey," she said. "You're that guy—don't go rushin' back there!"

"I won't," I promised. "Can you tell him I'm here, please?"

"Well, okay, but don't move or I'll sic Big Greg on you."

"Big Greg" must have been the kid who told her last time that he wasn't a bouncer.

"Oh, don't do that," I said. "I'll wait right here."

"You better." She looked at the people behind me. "I'll be right with ya."

She went back through the area where they prepared the food, then returned moments later.

"He says you can go back. You know the way. But walk around."

I wasn't looking forward to climbing over the counter again, so I went around and back to the office. Big Greg gave me a look, but that was all.

"Mr. Headston, what can I do for you?"

"I never did get a chance to talk to your employees."

"About Temp?" he asked.

"Yes, and now that he's been murdered, I need to do it more than ever."

"You're looking into his murder?"

"Yes."

"Isn't that the job of the police?"

"I've been asked by his wife."

"The wife he ran away from?"

"Yes."

He shook his head.

"I don't understand any of this," he said. "Why would someone want to kill him?"

"I don't know," I said. "But the only way I can find out is to ask questions."

"Of the people who work here?" he asked.

"And at his former job," I said. "But the offices are closed now, so I came here. Is this the shift he would have been working? I recognize the girl at the register."

"Yeah, he worked the same shift as Angie."

"And Big Greg?"

He grinned.

"Big Greg?" he asked. "Yeah, Greg, too."

"Okay," I said, "I'll talk to them."

"You can use my office," he offered, getting up from his desk. "I'll spell them so they can come in."

"Thank you."

"I want to do what I can to help find out who killed Temp," he said. "I liked him."

"I'll take Angie, first."

"Okay."

He went out. I sat behind his desk, and moments later the girl came in.

"Close the door," I said.

"I'd rather leave it open."

"All right. Have a seat."

She sat across from me. She was in her twenties, a little overweight with glasses and slightly buck teeth.

"Woodley says I gotta answer your questions."

"Did he tell you why?"

"Yeah, you're a private eye lookin' for whoever killed Temp."

"That's right."

"So that first day, when you asked about my break, you weren't comin' on to me."

"No," I said, "sorry."

She looked embarrassed.

"I wouldn't think a young, pretty girl would be interested in me, anyway."

She put her hand up to the back of her hair.

"I ain't so pretty." But she was obviously pleased I had said it.

"Let me just ask a few questions, and you can go back to work. Okay?"

She dropped her hand to her lap. "Okay."

I finished with Angie, then Greg came in. I asked them the same questions. How well did they know Temp? Did he talk about himself? Did he ever mention having a problem with anyone? Neither of them knew anything helpful. They both said he "kept to himself."

There were two other employees, both young boys. I spoke to them, and if anything, they knew even less.

When I was done, Woodley came back in.

"Was that any help?" he asked.

I came around his desk and stood in front of him.

"Not much, I'm afraid," I admitted. We shook hands. "Thanks."

"Let me know what happens, will you?" he asked.

"Sure."

I left his office, and the Burger World, probably for the final time.

CHAPTER TWENTY-EIGHT

I went home and took a shower. I could still smell Beth Munnings on me, and it didn't bring back good memories.

I got dressed again, this time in jeans and a T-shirt, rather than a suit, since I wasn't planning on going out. I was tired and wanted to make some notes on the case on my old home laptop. I sat, typed for about half an hour, then saved it to a flash drive. When I got to my office, I'd transfer the drive to my office laptop, so that the case notes were all in the same machine.

I was hungry, but still didn't want to go out, so I called and had some Chinese delivered. While I was waiting for it, there was a knock on my door. It was too soon for it to be the delivery man. When I opened it and saw Ally there, I was surprised.

"Hi, private eye!" she said, brightly.

"How did you find me?" I asked.

"You're listed," she said. "I just looked you up."

"What are you doing here?"

"Can't I come in?"

"Ally...how old are you?"

"Twenty-three," she said. "Headstone, I'm not hittin' on you."

"Yeah, okay," I said, "come on in."

I let her pass, closed the door, turned to find her looking the place over.

"So?" I asked. "Does it pass inspection?"

"It's cool," she said, "because it's you—simple."

"Thanks. You want to tell me what brings you here?"

"Can I take off my jacket?" It was just a short jean jacket. I wondered how she could dress the way she did in the cold.

"Sure."

She removed it and dropped it on a chair. Beneath she was—as usual—sleeveless to show off her tattoos.

"Have a seat," I invited her.

She sat down on top of her jacket. I sat on the sofa.

"What's up, Ally?"

"I want to help you."

"You have," I said. "And I appreciate it."

"That was when Mr. Kessenger was missin'. Now he's dead. I want to help more," she said. "I wanna work for you."

"We talked about this," I said. "I can't pay you—"

"Screw that," she said. "Let's say I'd be...an apprentice. I'll learn the trade from you. I'll become a lady P.I., like...Honey West."

"What do you know about Honey West?" I asked.

"Hey, I watch reruns."

I studied her for a few moments. I still hadn't gotten up to Herman James to talk to the employees, but Ally knew some of them.

"How long were you working at Herman James?"

"Just a few months," she replied, "but I made sure I got to know people. I like to experience my life, and that means—you know—mixin' in."

"Okay, then," I said. "I want you to tell me about

some of the people there. Preferably, people who Kessenger dealt with."

"I can do that!" she said, happily. "But...you got anythin' to eat around here?"

Right at that moment the doorbell buzzed from downstairs.

"How'd you get up here without me buzzing you in?"

"A cute young guy," she said. "He lives below you, I think."

I went to the door and pressed the intercom.

"Chinese take-out," a voice said.

"Come on up." I buzzed him in.

"There, I said, turning to face her, "food. Any other requests?"

CHAPTER TWENTY-NINE

Luckily, I ordered enough for two. I always do. That's why I had a growing midsection as I hit fifty.

"...and then there's Fancy Whitfield."

"Fancy?"

"Her name's Felicia, but everybody calls her Fancy."

"Why?"

"You'll know when you meet her," she said, around a mouthful of pork lo mein.

"And who else?"

"He was always fighting with Mr. Walcott."

"His partner."

She nodded.

"They didn't get along very well."

"What did they argue about?"

"I don't know, exactly," she said. "They always made sure to yell at each other behind closed doors."

"Anyone else?"

"Dan Cushing and Vincent Lorenzo."

"And they are?"

"A couple of traders," she said. "They weren't pullin' their weight. Walcott wanted to fire them, but they thought it was Mr. Kessenger talkin' against them."

"Why'd they think that?"

"I don't know," she said. "Maybe somebody told them."

"How do you know all this?" I asked.

"I told you," she said. "I listen."

"At the water cooler?"

She smiled.

"Water cooler, lunch, smoking break—"

"Why?"

"What?"

"Why were you listening?"

"See these tattoos?" she asked.

"I see," I said. "I don't understand them, but I see them."

"I got them in my youth," she said, "my misspent youth."

"Your—you're twenty-three."

"I was eighteen when I got my first tattoo—this one." She pointed to a pentagram on one arm. "Twenty when I got this one."

She pointed to a wolf on her right arm. "By the time I was twenty-one I had several more, some that you can't see."

"And then?"

"And then I realized what mistakes I'd made gettin' them," she said. "So I atone by dressing to show them. I was dumb enough to get them, why not show people just how dumb? I also dropped out of college. Another mistake. So now I have to better myself in other ways."

"By listening."

She nodded. "And learning all I can, wherever I am. I've had several jobs, in law firms, publishing, Wall Street—and now I wanna learn from you."

I sat back and stared at her for a few long seconds.

"Okay," I said, then, "but first I need some more information."

"Wait a minute." She leaned back and dug into the pocket of her jeans. She came out with piece of paper and passed it to me.

"What's this?" I asked.

"Those are the phone numbers you wanted me to check for you," she said.

I'd forgotten about them. That was back when Kessenger was missing, not dead. I looked at it, saw a list of names and addresses.

"I gave you the ones he called the most," she said, going back to the food.

"Okay." I folded it and put it in my pocket. "This'll probably still help, but I am going to need some more information about the Herman James crew."

She looked down at the containers on the coffee table between us.

"You want that last egg roll?" she asked.

CHAPTER THIIRTY

The employees at Herman James lied.

But before I get to that, Ally and I finished our dinner, and went over and over the employees at Herman James. She was a sharp cookie and had an opinion and comment about most of the major players in the company, and some of the minor ones.

After we finished, we killed a six-pack of beer I'd had in the fridge for a while, and then she left.

"I'll come into the office tomorrow," she said, at the door.

"Here." I took my office key from my pocket. "I'll be stopping at Herman James first thing in the morning. You go to the office and let yourself in."

"And what do I do when I get there?"

"Pick out a desk," I said. "Answer the phone. Wait for me."

"That's it?"

"For now. I'll come up with more for you to do."

"Cool," she said. "So now I'm a lady P.I.?"

"Not yet," I said. "You'll have to do a few years under me, and then we can get you your own license."

"A few years?"

"At least," I said. "If you're up to it."

"Oh, I'm up for it," she said. "I'm not gettin' any younger, ya know."

"That makes two of us."

I got to Herman James at 9 a.m.

"Tiffany," I said to the girl out front. "Good morning."

According to Ally, Tiffany was not above giving blowjobs out in the conference rooms. Not to Kessenger, but to Walcott and enough of the other players in the company.

She stared up at me from behind her desk, trying to figure out if she knew me, or had seen me before.

"I'm here to see Mr. Walcott, again," I said, hoping that reminded her. After what Ally had told me, I couldn't help staring at her full-lipped mouth. I think I might have made her feel self-conscious.

"Yes, sir," she said, "if you'll just wait a moment."

She made her call, spoke briefly, and hung up.

"He says you'll know the way?"

"Yes, I will," I said. "Thank you, Tiffany. You look lovely today."

"Uh...thank you."

As I went down the hall, I could imagine her taking out her compact and checking her face in the mirror.

When I got to Walcott's office the door was open and he was waiting.

"Mr. Headston," he said, shaking my hand, "I'm not sure I thought we'd be seeing you again. I mean...Temp is dead, and aren't the police working on his...case?"

"They are," I said, "but I've been hired by Nancy Kessenger's lawyer to look into the matter."

"Nancy," he said, surprised. "Is she, uh, suspected

of…of something?"

"In a murder, Mr. Walcott, the surviving spouse is always the first suspect."

"I see." He started to go back around his desk.

"And then the partner."

He stopped short to look at me and see if I was joking.

"The partner," he said, seating himself, "Well, I'm his partner. Or, I was."

"That's right."

He finally got it and his eyes widened.

"You mean…they suspect me?"

"They suspect you," I said, "I suspect you. I'm here so you can convince me of your innocence."

"How can I do that?"

"What'd you tell the cops?"

"That I was home," he said, "with my wife."

"Your wife?" I said. "I didn't know you were married."

"Yes," he said, "happily for fourteen years."

"Is that so?" I said. "How long, totally?"

"Very funny. We've been married fourteen years."

"What's your wife's name?"

"Laura."

"Does Laura know about the blowjobs in the conference rooms from Tiffany?"

He paled.

"What?"

"Or does she come in here and do you, since you're the boss?"

"Now, listen here—"

"That kind of talk can spoil a perfect marriage, even if it's not true, don't you think?"

He shifted in his seat.

"What do you want, Headston?"

"What made Kessenger walk away from this company? And was it something that could've gotten him killed?"

"I don't know the answer to either one of those questions."

"Oh, yeah, you do," I said. "You know why he walked away. What was the problem up here? Too much sex and drugs, or what?"

The sex I'd heard about from Ally. The drugs were a guess. Tiffany looked like a real party girl, to me.

"Jesus, you can't talk like that!" Walcott said.

"Well," I said, "not to your wife, and not to the cops but hey, it's just you and me here, bud."

"All right, look," Walcott said, "Temp found out that I had some, uh, business practices that weren't entirely on the level."

"You were breaking the law?"

"Well, let's just say the FCC wouldn't be very happy with the practices."

"So you were bending the rules, and he didn't like it."

He nodded. "You could say that, yeah."

"So why does he walk away and get a job in Burger World? Why not buy you out, or sell his half of the business to you?"

"He might've gotten around to that," Walcott said. "I think he was taking the time to think."

"What about his wife?" I asked.

"He was thinking about that, too," Walcott guessed. "I knew neither of them were happy."

"How long had they been married?" I asked, wondering why I hadn't asked either one of them that question.

"I'm not sure, fifteen, maybe sixteen years."

"And who were his professional enemies?"

"Enemies?" Walcott repeated. "We're not spies, Mr. Headston. We don't have enemies—"

"Well, not per se," I said, cutting him off, "but who were your professional rivals?"

"Well...everybody, from Edward James to Merrill Lynch. We're all after the same things."

"Were you friends, Mr. Walcott," I asked. "You said you were partners, which was obvious. But how about friends?"

He thought a moment.

"In the beginning, yes, we were friends," he said. "We even ate out with our wives along. But...not so much, lately. There's been too much water under and over the bridge."

"But not enough to kill for?"

"Certainly not!"

"All right," I said, "I'll need an office to use to talk to your employees."

"All of them?"

"Didn't the police question all of them?"

"Well, yes, but—"

"I'm working for Nancy Kessenger, Mr. Walcott," I said. "I believe that should give me a little—no, a lot of leeway, and cooperation."

He looked pained.

"Very well," he said, "I'll set you up in one of the small conference rooms."

I didn't ask him if it would be one of Tiffany's conference rooms.

CHAPTER THIIRTY-ONE

Tiffany was the first one in so I got right down to it.

"Did you have sex with Templeton Kessenger?"

"No!"

"I'm not going to ask if you've had sex with anyone else," I said. "You're a good-looking girl—single?"

"What? Yes, I'm single. And, uh, thank you."

"But you're also in a good position to hear things," I said, "like gossip, right?"

"Well, yes."

"Give me some."

"Gossip?"

"About Temple Kessenger," I said. "Who was he sleeping with, who hated him, who did he hate—"

"He didn't hate anybody," she said. "He was a nice man. The only one up here who didn't..." She trailed off, not knowing how to put it.

"Disrespect you?"

Her eyes brightened.

"That's it! He didn't disrespect me."

"And the other men in the office do?"

"Not just the men," she muttered.

"What about him?" I asked. "Did anyone disrespect him?"

"The young guys up here," she said, "always had something to say about the partners."

"Young guys? Like Dan Cushing and Vincent Lorenzo?"

"How did you hear about them?"

"I have eyes and ears all over," I told her. "That's my job."

She didn't seem to like that, and hunched her shoulders, a bit.

"Well, yeah, those two, and others. Bill Rutledge especially."

"What about Rutledge?"

"He's been here for years and thinks he should've been a partner by now," she said. "He says it was Mr. Kessenger keepin' him down."

"And the other two? Who do they blame?"

"Everybody!"

"What about Fancy Whitfield?"

"My God!" she said, hugging herself, now, as if trying to hide. "You do have eyes and ears."

"What was her relationship with Mr. Kessenger?"

"Felicia was always throwing herself at him," she said. "She's thirty now and starting to panic."

"So she figured if she got involved with the boss—"

"—he'd move her up the ladder. But she was barkin' up the wrong tree."

"So Mr. Walcott wouldn't've moved her up?"

"I don't know about that," she said, "but he'd have sex with her in a minute. He'd fuck a...a...well, anythin'!"

"Does he use his position to get the female employees to sleep with him?"

"Let's just say he spends a lot of time in his office

with the door locked," she said, rubbing her arms, now, as if trying to clean something off.

"The women up here should have more respect for themselves," I commented.

"Yeah," she muttered, "I guess."

"Okay, Tiffany," I said, "thanks for coming in."

She stood up wordlessly and walked out, a little unsteady. Maybe she thought I was going to be much meaner, more aggressive. Well, that might come later. But now I needed to get a feel for the employees.

Walcott was in charge of sending them in, so in rapid succession I got to talk to a few more of the ladies. Kessenger was a gentleman, Walcott was a louse and a sexual predator and also some of the male employees. Finally I got to the three men I'd heard about: Cushing, Lorenzo and Rutledge.

Cushing and Lorenzo were young lions, late twenties or so, and both complained that Kessenger and Walcott were keeping them down. They came in one after the other.

"Why don't you leave?" I asked Cushing.

"You kiddin'? I got four years invested in this place."

Lorenzo said he had three.

"Who do you think was keeping you down, Walcott or Kessenger?"

Cushing said, "Kessenger. He doesn't like the younger men in the company."

Lorenzo wasn't so quick to answer.

"Wait a minute," he said. "You're investigatin' his murder, right? You can't pin that on me. I worked my way up from the streets, man." I could tell, because his suit was ill-fitting. He had broad shoulders, and big hands, and looked like he belonged in the ring, rather than on Wall Street. But I had to give him credit for working his way up.

"I know how you cops work," he said.

"I'm not a cop," I said. "I'm a private investigator."

"Same difference," he said. "You're even worse, because you P.I.s don't have any rules to break."

Cushing didn't care whether I was a cop or a P.I.

"They both wanted to keep me down, but that Kessenger—what a phony. Wanted everybody to think he was such a gentleman and all. You know what I think?"

"No, what do you think?"

"Ah," he said, waving his hand, "I ain't gonna say."

Lorenzo may have looked like he came from the streets, but Cushing talked like it. Or it might have just been his Brooklyn accent.

Since Lorenzo came in after Cushing I said, "Your buddy Cushing thinks Kessenger was trying to keep him down. He had no qualms about badmouthing both partners."

"Well, Kessenger's dead, but if that gets back to Walcott, he gets fired, right?"

"What do you think of Cushing."

He made a rude sound with his mouth, shrugged and said, "Ah, he's a fag."

He wouldn't say much more after that, so I didn't know if he meant, literally, that Cushing was gay.

Bill Rutledge came in after them. Ten years older, and he looked to have every year of it on his face. The other two had kept their suit jackets on, but Rutledge was in shirt sleeves, rolled up almost to his biceps.

"Is this about Kessenger?" he demanded, as soon as he walked in.

"It is," I said. "Why? You got something to tell me?"

"I've got nothing to say about Temple Kessenger," Rutledge said, sitting down like he was lounging. The other employees had all sat up straight, nervously. Even Lorenzo and Cushing, who were trying to look cool the whole time.

"Why not?"

"We weren't friends," he said. "We didn't really work together."

"How do you mean?"

"I report to Walcott," Rutledge said, "plain and simple."

"But they're partners."

"It doesn't matter," Rutledge said. "I took this job on the condition I only reported to Walcott. If you want to know anymore, talk to him." He stood up to leave.

"I'll do that," I said. "Maybe he can give me a good motive for you."

"Motive?" He stopped short of the door, turned back. "Whoa, whoa, buddy. You talking about a motive to kill Kessenger? Why the hell would I do a thing like that? Okay, maybe I didn't like the guy, but that's no reason to kill him."

"I guess we'll see, Mr. Rutledge," I said "Thanks for coming in."

"Hey, look—"

"That's all, Mr. Rutledge," I said. "I have other people to talk to."

CHAPTER THIIRTY-TWO

I talked to some other employees, but the ones who interested me the most were Walcott, Rutledge, Cushing and Lorenzo. I decided to have one more conversation with Walcott before I left.

"Tell me about Rutledge," I said sitting in his office, again.

"Why? What did he tell you?"

"Not much. He said I'd have to talk to you about him. Apparently, you and he have some deal."

"Deal?"

"Yeah, something about him not having to report to Kessenger, but only you?"

"Oh, yeah, that. Well, he was my man. I recruited him to come work for us."

"And did Kessenger do that, too?" I asked. "Recruit people?"

"Hell, no," Walcott said. "If it was up to him it would have just been him and me, all these years. Temp wasn't a big thinker."

"But I thought it was his thinking that made this a successful business."

"His techniques, yes," Walcott said. "But I grew this company to what it is today."

"Without his help?"

"I told you," Walcott said, testily, "we used his techniques, but recruiting personnel, growing this business, that was all me."

"What about Mrs. Kessenger?"

"What about her?"

"Has she ever met Rutledge? Or the other two?"

"Are you thinking she was sleeping with one of them?" Walcott asked. "That's preposterous."

"You mean she didn't cheat?"

"Not with anyone from here," Walcott said. "Maybe she had somebody out at that country club she goes to."

"You mean like a tennis pro or a Pilates instructor?"

"Why not?" he asked. "That makes more sense than her sleeping with anybody from this company."

"Why did you recruit Rutledge?"

"What?" Walcott seemed distracted by the talk of Nancy Kessenger possibly cheating.

"Rutledge. What was it about him made you want him in the company?"

"Oh, I, uh, thought he was a go-getter."

"And were you right?"

"He's been very successful, so I suppose I was."

"And how long has he worked here?"

"About three years. Look, why the interest in Bill Rutledge?"

"He wasn't very forthcoming," I said. "I wondered why?"

"He does his job," Walcott said. "That's all I ever cared about."

I made a mental note to ask Ally some more about Bill Rutledge.

"All right, Mr. Walcott," I said, "I think I've got

what I need."

He gave me a surprised look.

"You know who the killer is?"

"Oh, no," I said, "I just meant I have all the information I need about your employees. It'll take some time for me to make an assessment."

"And once you do? Then what?"

"I'll give whatever I come up with to the police."

He raised his hands and dropped them.

"So then they'll be back!"

"I'm sure they will," I said.

"When will this end?" he asked, shaking his head.

"When we know who killed Templeton Kessenger, Mr. Walcott," I answered, "and not before."

CHAPTER THIIRTY-THREE

I had spent a good part of the workday up at Herman James, so when I got back to the office, I brought two sandwiches with me, in case Ally hadn't eaten.

She looked up from the desk she had picked out, and smiled when I walked in. She had her Dell laptop open and in front of her.

"Have you eaten anything?" I asked.

"For lunch, yes," she said "for dinner, no."

I put the bag down on the desk and took out two sandwiches wrapped in wax paper.

"Two roast beef sandwiches, one with mayo, one without, because I didn't know how you liked it."

"Without, please."

"Good," I said handing it to her, "because I like it with."

I also took out two cans of Coke.

"Diet or regular?" I asked.

"Regular."

I also drank regular but I gave it to her.

"What did you find out today?" Ally asked me. "Come up with any clues?"

"I talked to a lot of people," I told her. "A lot of what you told me came in handy."

"About Tiffany?" she asked. "That cold bitch. I don't see why anybody wants a blowjob from her. If they stick it in her mouth it'd freeze and fall off."

"I thought she was a nice girl."

She stopped chewing and stared at me.

"Aw, you're kiddin' me," she finally said. Then she frowned. "Or did she—"

"No, no," I said, "she didn't. "But she was pretty forthcoming, once I let her know I was aware of some things she didn't want people to know."

She pointed her finger at me and said proudly, "I understood that!"

I took a big bite, chewed and swallowed, washed it down with some Diet Coke without making a face.

"So, who do you think did it?" she asked.

"I haven't gotten that far, yet," I said, "but there are some men who interest me, mainly Rutledge and Walcott."

"Oh, them," she said. "They're like two peas in a pod, only..." She paused to take a bite.

"Only what?"

She held up her hand and waved for me to wait a moment while she chewed.

"There's somethin' off about that relationship," she finally said.

"Like what?"

"I don't know, just somethin'...off."

"You think they're gay?"

"No, no, that ain't it," she said shaking her head. "Rutledge used to come in late, take late lunches, bug all the girls. It always bothered Mr. Kessenger, but he never said anythin'."

"Why not?"

"Because Rutledge was Mr. Walcott's man."

I chewed and thought about it.

"You think Rutledge had something on Walcott?"

"Whataya mean, like blackmail?"

I nodded.

"I dunno, maybe," she said. "That would explain why he could get away with anything he wanted."

"Yeah, but even so, it wouldn't explain killing Temple Kessenger. So even if it's true, one's got nothing to do with the other."

We finished eating and she cleaned up the garbage, tossed it in a can.

"Hope you don't mind I took this desk. It's closest to your office."

"That's okay. The last person who had that desk was a real good detective."

Actually, the last person who had that desk was fat and lazy, had a heart attack and died slumped over it, but I didn't want to tell her that.

"You know," I said, "I'd really like to know where Walcott and Rutledge live, see if they're anywhere in the vicinity of Kessenger's new place. I'm going to have to hunt those addresses up, maybe use Mrs. Kessenger's lawyer—"

"Here ya go," she said, handing me a piece of paper she had just written on. I saw two addresses there, with "Walcott" and "Rutledge" written above them.

"Where did you get these?" I asked. "And when?"

"My laptop," she said. "Before I left Herman James I made a point of hacking their personnel files and copying them to my hard drive."

"That was…brilliant," I said.

"Careful with the compliments, boss," she said.

"You might have to start payin' me in somethin' other than sandwiches."

"I wish I could," I said.

"Well, if you give me your email I'll send the whole file to your computer."

"I'll give it to you, but my machine is pretty old. I only hope I can open the file."

"If you can't, let me know. I should be able to make some adjustments. Is it here? In your office?"

"Yeah, on my desk," I said. "But you've done enough for one day. Just send me the email and I'll let you know if there's a problem."

"Well, okay," she said. "I am kinda tired. I'll pack up and take off."

"I'll be here, so I'll see you in the morning, Ally." I waved the addresses. "Thanks for this."

I went into my office and closed my door, then stared balefully at the old Dell computer on my desk. It was over ten years old, and I'd already had plenty of problems trying to read files that people have sent me from newer machines. I guess I was embarrassed to let Ally see it, since she seemed to have herself a new, state of the art laptop.

Of course, I was going to have to stop being embarrassed about anything if I was going to be teaching her the ropes. The important stuff is not all the new devices the bigger agencies are using—computers, cell phones, apps—it's one in here (head) and here (heart). And she was a pretty sharp cookie for someone so young. Plus, I liked her. She'd be good to have around, to keep me on my toes. And she was a kid while I was a fat old man, so there was no danger of any hanky-panky, if they still called it that. With all the sexual harassment suits being brought against the likes of Bill Cosby, Harvey Weinstein, Kevin Spacey and others—and the "Me, too" movement it started— men weren't even going to be able to give women compliments, anymore.

But I wasn't going to have to worry about that with Ally. All I was going to have to worry about was the student surpassing the teacher.

CHAPTER THIIRTY-FOUR

I got up the next morning, put on a pot of coffee and considered my options. Kessenger could have been killed because of something in his personal life, or his professional life, at Herman James, or at Burger World.

If it was personal, then his wife moves right to the top of the list.

If it was professional, then the suspect comes from the employee list of Herman James.

What were the chances that, in the short time he'd worked at Burger World, Temple Kessenger made somebody mad enough to want to kill him?

I had to disqualify Burger World. It didn't make sense that he got somebody's shift, and they killed him for it. It just didn't scan.

On the way to work I picked up coffee and bagels, which was something one of us used to do when I was running a fully outfitted agency.

When I entered, Ally was at her staked out desk—which I now had to start thinking of as her desk.

"Good morning," I said.

"'Mornin', boss."

I gave her the coffee and set the bag of six bagels down on the desk.

"They're all buttered," I said, "I hope that's okay."

"It's fine."

I snagged a sesame seed one for myself and took it into my office. I left the door open, since I'd decided not to try to hide my aged computer from her.

She came to the door, holding her breakfast in her hands.

"What's on the agenda for today?" she asked, leaning against the door jamb.

"I'm going to look a little deeper into Rutledge and Walcott today," I said. "Meanwhile, maybe you could do a little of your computer magic and get me some info on the other two, Cushing and Lorenzo?"

"Sure thing. What kind of stuff?"

"Background, if they have any arrests or any kind of a record?"

"Got it."

Then I made a command decision.

"And you might want to look at this old relic and see if you can clean it up, get it to operate a little faster," I said, "since I can't afford to buy a new one, right now."

"I'll be your own person geek squad," she promised.

I noticed she was wearing a long-sleeved top, along with a pair of jeans and flat shoes.

"And Ally, this isn't Herman James," I said. "You don't have to dress to cover up the tattoos."

"Oh, that's okay," she said. "That ain't for you, it's for me. After hearin' myself say some things to you out loud, I started thinkin'. Why not over them up?"

"Gotcha," I said.

She went back to her desk. I was about to get up and leave when my cell phone went off. (It played a chime. You really can't say your phone "rang," anymore, and I didn't have any fancy ring tone for it.)

"Headstone Agency," I said.

"Mr. Headstone, this is Seymour Griffith, from Griffith, Wymouth and Estevez?"

"I remember," I assured him. "Nancy Kessenger's lawyer."

"Exactly. I wonder if you could meet me down at the Tombs in an hour."

The Tombs was the nickname for the Manhattan Detention Complex in lower Manhattan, on White Street.

"I can be there, if it's an emergency."

"Oh, it is, I assure you," he said. "The detectives have arrested Nancy Kessenger for killing her husband."

CHAPTER THIIRTY-FIVE

I waited with Griffith while Nancy Kessenger was brought to a visitor's room so we could talk with her.

"They came and got her this morning," he said, "rousted her out of bed and dragged her down here before giving her a chance to call me."

"Was this Detectives Leon and Stokes?"

"Yes, apparently accompanied by a car from the White Plains authorities."

A corrections officer came over to tell us she was ready. When we entered the room, she was seated at a table, handcuffed, already clad in an orange jumpsuit. She wasn't behind glass, because this was a consultation with her attorney and, by association, me.

There were two chairs set up across from her. They were the same color as the walls and the table, grey.

"Have a seat," Griffith said to me. He sat and I sat beside him.

"Mr. Headston," Nancy said. "I'm glad to see you."

"Mrs. Kessenger," I said, "I'm sorry it's under these circumstances."

"That's all right," she said. "These policemen don't know any better. Arrest the wife for the husband's murder."

"What a cliché, huh?" I asked.

She nodded. Without her perfect make-up she had aged at least five years. The jumpsuit was baggy on her, so I couldn't see the Pilates figure. Still, she'd be considered a yummy morsel on the inside.

She looked at Griffith and said, "When do I get out, Griff?"

"You heard the judge, Nancy," Griffith said. "No bail for first degree murder."

"Why first degree?" I asked. "It looked to me like Kessenger could've been killed in a fight."

"The M.E. says Kessenger was strangled from behind, never saw it coming," Griffith said. "The D.A. says that's first degree."

"So how do we get Mrs. Kessenger out?"

"I'm working on it," he said, then looked at her and repeated himself.

"Well, work faster," she said. "I feel like a piece of meat, in here. I've already fended off two amorous advances. And call me Nancy, Mr. Headston."

I was impressed. Nancy Kessenger seemed to be tougher than I would have thought, not the pampered, middle-aged matron I assumed she was.

Griffith went over his plans and strategy with Nancy while I listened. I had some questions of my own for her, but I wanted to ask them when we were alone. I had a feeling there might be some things she didn't want to discuss in front of her lawyer.

On the other hand, I was wondering why he wanted me there. Now that she had been arrested, I would have thought he'd bring in his big guns, his firm's investigators.

"All right," he told her, "just sit tight, try to stay out of trouble, and we'll be back to get you out."

He reached out to touch her hand, a reassuring gesture, and then stood up. I walked with him to the door but stopped there.

"Do you mind if I have a few minutes with her alone?" I asked.

"Not at all," he said. "I'll wait outside."

He knocked, was allowed out, and I went and sat back down across from Nancy.

"What is it, Mr. Headston?"

"If I'm to call you Nancy, you might as well call me John."

"Or Johnny?" she asked, with a wan smile.

"If you like."

"My first boyfriend's name was Johnny," she said. "I'll call you that."

"Fine," I said.

"What's on your mind, Johnny?"

"I'm wondering if you had any contact with your husband between the time I told you where he was, and the time he was killed?"

"Not very much."

"What does that mean?"

"Well, I contacted him," she said, "but he didn't want to see me or talk to me."

"Did he say why?"

"He said something very strange," she answered. "He said it was for my own good."

"Anything else?"

She shook her head. "He wouldn't elaborate. I got the feeling he thought he was...protecting me."

"Against what?"

"I haven't the slightest."

"Do you know if he received any threats leading up

to his disappearance?"

"No," she said. "That is, I don't know if he did, but I also don't know if he didn't. Does that make sense?"

"It does. Okay," I said, "if your husband felt threatened by someone, who would he talk to about it? Did he have a friend he'd use as a confidante?"

"Not that I know of."

"Did you have another couple you had as friends, had dinner with?"

"No."

"Did you guys have any kind of a life together?"

"Not for a very long time."

"And why was that?"

"We grew apart. Couples do that."

"I guess." I'd never been married, so I could only guess.

"Johnny," she said, reaching out to touch my hand in an assuring gesture, "I have faith that you'll prove I didn't do this." She had to use both hands, since she was cuffed.

"I'm going to do my best, Nancy." I said, "but before I go, I need to ask you one more thing."

"What is it?" She took her hands back.

"Were you seeing anyone else at the time your husband left?"

She hesitated, then said, "No, not at the time he left."

"Okay, that was a very precise answer," I said. "Let's try again. Have you ever cheated on your husband, before he left, after he left, or after he was killed?"

"If it was after he was killed," she said, "then it wasn't cheating, right?"

"Right."

"All right," she said. "Then that one."

"I'll need his name and address."

"He's not involved in this."

"Can he give you an alibi?"

"No."

"Did he know your husband?"

"No, he never met him."

"So he wasn't a friend or colleague of your husband's."

"Of course not."

"Nancy," I said. "It's only been a matter of days since your husband was killed. How did this happen?"

"I was in need of comfort," she said. "And he was there. It just…happened."

"So it's not a relationship."

"No, no," she said, "we just fucked." She pinned me with a steady gaze. "If you had been there at that moment, it might have been you, Johnny."

I pushed that comment to the side.

Out in the hall Griffith asked, "Did you get what you needed?"

"I think so."

"Come on, let's get out of here."

We walked to his car, and then I asked him the question that had been on my mind.

"Why me?"

"What?"

"Now that she's been arrested, I thought you'd bring in your top men," I said. "Why me?"

"Because, Mr. Headston," he said, "you have a head start. My men would have to go over ground you've already covered. I can't waste that time."

"I see."

"Don't worry," he said. "You'll be paid what they get paid."

"I wasn't worried about that."

"Besides," he said, opening his rear car door and tossing his briefcase in, "I checked you out."

"You did?"

"Of course," he said. "At one time you were at the top of this game. You had a twelve-man agency of your own, and that was when you were pretty young."

"Don't you want to know what happened?"

"I know what happened," he said, opening his driver's side door.

"And?"

"It could happen to anybody," he said, getting into the car. "Keep me posted on your investigation, and I'll let you know when I get her out."

"Okay," I said.

"Here," he said, opening his window and holding something out to me.

"What is it?" I asked, accepting it.

"A retainer," he answered. "To help you with the investigation."

He started his car and pulled away. I wondered why he didn't offer me a ride.

CHAPTER THIIRTY-SIX

When I got back to the office Ally asked, "Is she still in jail?"

"She is," I said. "The D.A. is going for murder one. No bail."

I pulled over a chair from one of the other desks and sat across from her.

"I cleaned out your computer," she said. "Got rid of some of the cookies, cleaned out the cache—"

"That's okay. I don't know what any of that means."

"It means your old HP computer is faster, now," she said, "but still a relic."

"What," I said to her, "do you know about the wives at Herman James?"

"Wow," she said, sitting back. "I heard some talk about wives while I was there, but mostly it was men complainin' about them, or braggin' about them."

"So tell me," I said, "who bragged and who complained."

"Lemme think."

"No, don't think," I said, sitting back. "Just talk..."

She talked.

* * *

Cushing bragged about his wife; Lorenzo complained about his. Regina Cushing was a nympho; Mary Lorenzo was a ball buster. Cushing's wife liked having threesomes with her husband and other women; Lorenzo's wife kept his balls in a jar by the bed.

"Which one do you believe?"

"Lorenzo," she said. "He's a sad man."

"And Cushing?"

"A braggart. He was always trying to get Tiffany into bed."

"And did he?"

"I don't think so," she said. "Tiffany did the boss, and some supervisors. She did whoever could help her get ahead."

"What about Walcott's wife?"

"They're divorced," she said. "Before I even got there."

"Any of them ever hit on you?"

"They flirted," she said. "Nobody ever hit on me seriously."

"Why not?"

She shrugged.

"I'm not the type."

"The Tiffany type?"

"Right."

"And Walcott's wife," I said. "Is she still around?"

"I don't think so," she said. "He never talked about her that I heard."

"Did he ever get calls from her?"

"I don't know," she said. "I only answered Mr. Kessenger's phone."

"Who answered Walcott's phone?"

"Well, while I was there, he didn't have a secretary.

He interviewed some girls but didn't hire any. So Tiffany had to answer his phone."

"Tiffany, again," I said. "Tell me about her."

"She's a slut."

"Yes, but did she have a boyfriend away from work?"

"Not that I ever heard her talk about, but you know who you might ask."

"Who?"

"One of the other girls up there. Her name's Carol...something. Oh, wait." She tapped on some keys on her laptop, presumably bringing up the employee records for Herman James. "Ah Carol Whitney. She's a secretary. I used to run into her in the cafeteria, and the ladies' room."

"Was she friends with Tiffany?"

"I don't know if they're friends," Ally said, "but she was always defending Tiffany."

"Okay, I'll have to have a talk with her."

"So what did Mrs. Kessenger have to say for herself?" Ally asked. "She didn't confess, did she?

"No, but she did say something strange," I answered. "I asked if she'd talked to her husband after I told her where he was."

"And?"

"She did, once. But she says he warned her off."

"Warned her?"

"Yes," I said, "he told her not to try to get in touch with him again, for her own protection."

"Wow, that's a new one," she said. "I've heard 'it's not you, it's me,' but never 'I'm leavin' you for your own protection.'"

"I know," I replied. "That's why I said it was odd."

"What do you suppose he meant?"

"That's what I have to find out, in order to clear her. If Kessenger was afraid of somebody, or something, it's got to be connected to do with why he was killed."

I stood up and walked to my office.

"Are you gonna tell the police?" she called after me.

"Let them get their own leads," I called back. "This one's mine!"

CHAPTER THIIRTY-SEVEN

If I had a staff of investigators, I would have sent them out to White Plains to talk with the Kessenger's neighbors. But I only had Ally. I sat at my desk and thought about it for a little while. One of us could talk to people out there, while the other talked to people in his Manhattan neighborhood. I wondered if I was taking unfair advantage of her, but she did say she wanted to learn the business. And I needed to stay in town to check out the addresses of Rutledge and Walcott, not to mention maybe the other two as well, Cushing and Lorenzo. And I didn't want Ally running into them.

So White Plains it was for her.

"And what do I do?" she asked, excitedly.

"Talk to the neighbors, find out whatever you can about the Kessengers."

"How do I get out there?"

"The train," I said.

"What about Uber?"

"I have a Lyft account," I said. "Use that. I'll give you some money from petty cash."

"Petty cash" was my pocket, which was the amount usually in there. However, I had stopped on the way back at my bank, deposited Griffith's check, and kept some cash out.

"A car is a good idea," I said, handing her some money. "And this'll buy you lunch, as well."

"Thanks, boss!"

"Keep in touch with me along the way," I said. "And don't do anything but ask questions, understand?"

"I understand."

"Go!"

"I'm gone!"

After she left, I hoped I wasn't going to be sorry.

Nancy had just been arrested. That meant I had plenty of time to mount an investigation. It wasn't as if we were racing the clock to save her from the big house and the chair.

So I took time to canvas the area around Kessenger's Manhattan loft, hoping I wouldn't run into Beth Munnings, again. I didn't want to have to revisit the huge mistake of having slept with her.

I tried some of the businesses in the area—electronic stores, bars, restaurants, a movie theater, art galleries, but Kesssenger really hadn't lived in the neighborhood long enough to make an impression. That meant I didn't have a choice. I was going to have to go back to his building and talk to the other tenants.

Kessenger was dead, his wife was in jail. So his belongings were still in the evidence room of the police department—including his keys. With Nancy under arrest, I doubted there would still be a cop on the door of Kessenger's place. But before I could get into that loft again, I had to get into the building.

I thought about ringing Beth's bell, wondering if she

would even let me in. I waited a little while to see if a tenant would come along and unlock the front door. Of course, I would've had to convince them to let me enter, as well. But it was a moot point. Nobody came in or out. That left me no choice but to ring bells. But that was an old trick that people had caught onto, and no one buzzed me in.

That left Beth Munning's bell.

I rang and her voice came over the intercom.

"Who is it?"

"It's John Headston, Beth. I—"

She chuckled and said, "I knew you'd be back for more." That was all she said, and she buzzed me in.

CHAPTER THIIRTY-EIGHT

Beth's place was one of two on the second floor. I started on the first floor, knocking on the door of 1A. There was a middle-aged couple living there, who were only too happy to let me in and answer questions if it helped solve Kessenger's murder.

"We didn't know him," Mrs. Adelaide Turner said, "but he was our neighbor."

"Exactly," her husband, Byron, said. "So if we can help, go ahead and ask."

But their answers were no help at all. They didn't hear anything, didn't see anything, didn't know much about Kessenger, and had actually never exchanged a word with him.

Plus they weren't home that night.

I asked them about the tenant in 1B.

"Not there," Byron said. "He spends six months out of the year in Europe, and he's been there for two months."

So the first floor was a bust.

I went up the stairs instead of taking the elevator, bypassed floor two and went directly to three. I knew Beth would be looking out her peephole, waiting for me to show up. I wanted to put that off for as long as I could.

I went to 3A first, because that was the unit directly

beneath Kessenger's. The door was answered by an extremely attractive woman in her forties, with black hair shot with grey, a perfectly made up face despite the fact that she was wearing some sort of silky loungewear, and not dressed to go out. In her left hand she held a martini glass.

"Yes."

"My name is John Headston," I said. "I'm looking into the murder of your neighbor, directly above you? Temple Kessenger?"

"Yes," she said, "a horrible thing. Come right in, Officer."

She backed away and I entered, closing the door behind me.

"I'm having a martini," she said. "Would you like one Officer? Or Detective? Or can't you drink on duty?"

"I'm not a policeman, Miss—"

"Cortez," she said, "my name is Miranda Cortez."

"Miss Cortez," I said, "I'm a private detective working for the victims' wife."

"Then you're not on duty, so to speak. Drink?"

"I'm afraid not," I said.

"Then what can I do for you, Mr…"

"Headston?"

"Mr. Headston."

"I was wondering if you were home the night of the murder, and if you heard or saw anything."

"I was home that night," she said "as I am home most nights, thank you very much. And I told all this to the police." She frowned. "At least, I think they were the police."

She was just a bit more than tipsy, which meant I was likely catching her at just the right moment. Since it was still early afternoon, I couldn't help but wonder what the rest of her day would be like.

Her place was much the same set up as Kessenger's had been, but there was more furniture—living room, dining room, bedroom—and some folding screens were acting as walls.

She walked me to the living room and said, "Please. Have a seat."

She sat on the sofa, and since I'd been on Beth's sofa when she kissed me, I took one of the matching arm-chairs. Not that I thought I was that irresistible, I was just playing it safe.

"I told the police I didn't hear anyone being murdered upstairs."

"I was just wondering how well you knew Mr. Kessenger?"

"Hardly at all. He was new in the building."

"How long have you lived here?"

"Almost four years," she said. "I moved in just after my divorce. I bought this place with my settlement money."

"I see. Did you ever speak with him, at all?"

She thought a moment. "I think once, when we were both getting our mail."

"And you never saw anyone loitering, perhaps waiting to get into the building somehow?"

"You mean the way you did today?"

I smiled. "I was buzzed in."

"Oh? By who?"

"Actually, Elizabeth Munnings. We're...acquainted."

"Crazy Beth?"

"Is that what they call her?"

"They don't just call her that," she said, "everybody

in the building knows she is crazy. You might want to look into her as a suspect for your murder."

"Did she have a problem with Kessenger?"

"She has a problem with everyone," she said.

I could believe that.

"What about the other tenant on this floor?"

"Yeah, he has a real problem with Crazy Beth, since he lives right above her."

"Did he know Kessenger?"

"I don't think so," she said. "He's an artist, and rarely comes out during the day. Says he needs the light to work, so if he goes out, it's at night. He probably wasn't home when the murder happened."

"What's his name?"

"Henry Louis Devereaux."

"Is that his art name?"

She smiled. "Yes, he signs his stuff with three initials, 'HLD.' His name on his lease is Henry Davis."

"Will he answer his door if I knock?" I asked.

"That depends on how heavily into his new project he is. He paints and sculpts. Some days you can hear him working with power tools." She rolled her eyes. "That's when Crazy Beth comes running up here and starts banging on his door. That's one of his, right there."

She was indicating a statue about a foot and a half high that looked like Aphrodite. I walked over and studied it.

"Looks like its chipped on the base," I said, pointing.

She came over to examine it, standing close, smelling of martini and perfume. I decided I wouldn't have minded if she jumped me the way Beth had.

"I'll have to tell him. Maybe he can fix it."

"Are the two of you friends?" I asked. "Is that why

he gave this to you?"

"To tell you the truth, we had a little thing going for a while," she said, "since neither one of us leaves the building very often. But it's over now. I guess that was a going away gift, of sorts."

"Well," I said standing, "I guess that's all I need. Thanks for talking to me."

"You're quite welcome."

As she walked me back to the door, we passed the bedroom section of the floor plan, separated by expensive looking screens. I could see behind one and it looked like a clothes rack, with blouses and dresses hanging on it, and I thought I saw a couple of men's items—pants, and a jacket. I figured maybe Mrs. Cortez also got a lover in her settlement.

"Here's my card," I said, at the open door, "in case you remember something."

"'Headstone,'" she read. "Very clever."

"Thanks," I said. "I once thought so."

CHAPTER THIIRTY-NINE

It wouldn't do me any good to skip an apartment. I'd just have to come back another time, so I went across the hall and knocked on the door of artist Henry Louis Devereaux, aka Henry Davis.

When I got no answer I decided to pound on the door until he did answer, or until I was convinced he wasn't home. I didn't hear any noises from inside, no power tools, no cutting or carving noises. Of course, he could have been just painting.

I knocked again, then tried the doorknob.

"I should have told you," Miranda said, from her doorway, "he never locks his door."

"Thanks."

She went back inside her 3A.

I went into 3B.

"Hello?"

"Pizza man?" a voice called.

This apartment was broken up into four rooms, with real walls.

"Not the pizza man," I called.

"Chinese food? I'm in the studio!"

There was a big kitchen with shiny, stainless steel appliances, a bedroom and a living room. I followed the voice to the fourth room, where I found a man standing in front of an easel, paint brush in hand.

"Not Chinese food," I said, from the doorway. "Where did you order from?"

He looked at me, a stocky, muscular man in a wife beater T-shirt that had once been white, but now as tie-died from all the paint he had wiped on it. There were paintings scattered all around the room, leaning against the walls and each other, some facing out, some facing the walls. He used lots of colors. I didn't see any other sculptures, though, like the one Miranda had shown me. I spotted one painting, looked like a portrait, and thought I recognized the subject.

"I don't remember," he said. "Maybe Mexican."

"Sorry," I said, "no food. I knocked several times."

"I heard," he said, "but I was busy. What can I do for you?"

"Can you take five minutes from your work?"

He looked pained but set the brush down.

"Five minutes. You want a beer?"

"No thanks."

As he went past me into the kitchen, I noticed he was only about five-and-a-half feet tall. Considering what Miranda had told me, I thought they made an odd couple. Then again, she said they never went out, so who would know? He was pretty lucky for a while, but according to her, it was over.

He opened the big fridge and took out a bottle of Dos Equis. After twisting off the cap he took two deep swallows, then looked at me again.

"Four minutes," he said.

"I'm investigating the murder that took place up on the fourth floor the other night."

"Yeah, Kessenger," he said. "Too bad."

"Did you know him?"

"I knew him on sight," Devereaux said. "To say good morning to."

"When you were both getting your mail?"

"Nuh-uh," he said. "I don't think he was getting mail. Didn't live here long enough for that."

"I see."

"Have you talked to the others in the building?"

"Yes, I just came from seeing your neighbor across the hall."

"Miranda," he said, with a smile. "She's a little more than a neighbor."

"Is that so?"

"Yeah, she's my woman," he said. "That's why I leave the door unlocked, so she can come and go."

"Uh-huh."

"Why, did she say something?" He'd stopped smiling and was frowning, now.

"No, no, nothing," I said.

"You didn't try anything with her, did you?" he asked, puffing up his chest and glowering at me. "I wouldn't take kindly to that."

"Nope, not me," I said, shaking my head. "Strictly business." He may have been short, but he was wide and muscular. I wasn't looking forward to tangling with him.

"I thought I noticed a painting of her in your studio."

"Yeah, she posed for me. That's how we got together. I'm always looking for models. I saw her in the hall and asked her to pose. She agreed, and we went from there."

He studied me for a few seconds, probably still waiting to see if I was lying about trying anything with "his woman."

"I gotta get back to work," he finally said.

"Sure," I said, "thanks for talking to me."

"Let yourself out," he muttered, and took the bottle with him back to his studio.

I stepped out into the hall and paused, thought about knocking on Miranda's door again. Devereaux had said a thing or two that didn't jibe with what she told me. Apparently, he thought they still had a thing going. I guessed he was in for a big disappointment.

I decided to go downtown and check in with Detectives Leon and Stokes and see if they'd share what they had with me.

I tried to get out of the building without Beth Munnings seeing me, but she wasn't having any of it. She was waiting on two with her door open.

"There you are," she said. "I've been waitin' since you rang my bell. Are you comin' in?"

"Afraid not, Beth."

"What, afraid of a rerun? I know I got nasty last time, but I didn't mean what I said. You were pretty good."

"It wasn't professional, Beth," I said. "I'm sorry, but it's not going to happen again. No offense."

"So why'd you ring, just to get in?"

"I'm afraid so."

She crossed her arms beneath her chubby breasts, bent the knee of one of her stubby legs. Took me a minute to realize she was posing.

"Say, I talked to the guy above you, the artist?"

"Yeah, Devereaux," she said. "What about it?"

"Did he ever ask you to pose for him?"

"As a matter of fact he did, but nothin' happened. I

went in, he painted for a while, then told me to come back the next day. He never even tried anything. What's wrong with you men? I never went back. What a loser." She dropped her arms and unbent her leg. "In fact, you're all losers!" She backed up and slammed her door.

I left while I had the chance.

CHAPTER FORTY

I found Leon in the bullpen at his desk, but his partner's desk was deserted.

"He's around here somewhere," Leon said. "What's on your mind?"

"You arrested Nancy Kessenger."

"I figured you'd hear about that from her lawyer. Did they fire you?"

"Nope, I'm still on the job."

"And you want to know what we've got."

"That's right."

"Well, I'll tell you what," he said. "Ask your employer. Once the D.A. gives him all that we have, he can give it to you."

"That's not very cooperative of you."

"Well, suppose you give me what you've got," Leon said, "and then maybe I'll return the favor."

"Maybe?" I said.

"If your information's any good."

"What about professional courtesy?" I asked.

"Cop to private cop, you mean?"

"How about cop to ex-cop?"

"Ex-cop? When?"

"A long time ago."

"And what happened?" he asked, leaning back in his chair and looking up at me. "Did you lose your badge the way you lost your license?"

"You told me you checked me out," I reminded him. "You know all about me."

"Yeah, I do," he said. "Youngest to ever make detective in the department, the golden child quits a year later to open his own agency. Things go great, he builds the agency to a twelve-man operation and then, boom."

"Yeah," I said, "boom. That's old news, Detective."

"Once your suspension was up, how could you go back to work as a one-man operation? I probably would've crawled right into a bottle."

"No point in that, Leon," I said. "I like this work, and I'm just happy to be able to keep on doing it. The rest of that stuff is behind me."

"Well, I gotta give you credit," Leon said. "I'd be an angst-ridden mess."

"Come on, what about it?" I asked. "I don't happen to think the wife did it."

"Well, she's got motive, she was in the city that night."

"What motive?"

"The angry wife."

"You got a murder weapon?"

He hesitated, then said, "No, that we don't have."

"What does the M.E. think it was?"

"Something blunt and heavy."

"Heavy? And you think the wife swung it?"

"You've seen her," Leon said. "The lady stays in shape."

"Okay, Detective," I said. "Thanks."

Yeah, for nothing.

* * *

I left the bullpen, took the elevator down to the lobby. They still managed to keep a few phone booths there, I sat in one and used my cell. I had a contact in the M.E.'s office from the old days. I just didn't know if the guy was still talking to me.

"Johnny Headstone," he said. "It's been years."

"Yeah, it has, Max. How you been?"

"Good. Still got the same job, but it ain't so bad. How are you doin', Johnny? I gotta tell you, I never believed all that shit that went down about you years ago. You still in the business?"

"Still got my license, Max," I said, "and I'm still working."

"So this ain't a social call."

"Not exactly. I haven't called you because—well, I figured you might not want me to."

"Well, you figured wrong. What can I do for ya?"

"You got a body about a week ago, maybe a little more. Templeton Kessenger is the name."

"I remember that one. Didn't they just arrest the wife?"

"That's right. I'm working the case for her lawyer."

"What do you need from here, Johnny?"

"I talked to Detective Leon and he wouldn't give me much. He said the murder weapon was a blunt instrument of some kind. I just need to know if there's anything else about it."

"Okay, hang on. I'm here alone, so I can pull a file."

"Thanks, Max."

I waited a few minutes, watching people walk back and forth in the police plaza lobby. They needed to identify themselves and say who they wanted to see to get any further.

"Johnny? The report says he was struck with a blunt instrument over twenty-seven times."

"Jesus," I said, "somebody was mad at him."

"I guess that's why they figure the wife. It also says he must've been killed by the first or second blow."

"Okay, Max. Listen, can I give you my cell number in case you find out anything else?"

"Sure."

I'd called the morgue landline, so he had to write the number down.

"Johnny, before you hang up, I've got one more thing."

"What's that?"

"They found something in the victim's head wounds and bagged it."

"What was it?"

"According to this," Max said, "they found microscopic bits of clay."

"Clay?"

"That's right. Must've come off the murder weapon."

"Clay," I said, again. "Thanks, Max."

"Any time, Johnny."

"Same price, Max?"

"Inflation, Johnny."

"It's on the way," I promised, and hung up.

Clay, I thought.

The kind that Henry Lewis Devereaux used in his sculptures? The kind that was missing from the base of that statue Miranda Cortez had?

That was what I had to find out.

CHAPTER FORTY-ONE

"Nothin'!" Ally complained. "I spent all day in that neighborhood and nobody told me anythin' about the Kessengers."

"No gossip?" I asked. "I find that hard to believe."

"Most of the neighbors said that everyone there kept to themselves. That if they wanted to talk to somebody, they'd go to their country club, not their neighbor's house." She shook her head. "Rich people!"

"Well," I said, "I'm sure you did your best."

I was sitting at my desk and she was standing in the doorway. It was already taking on the feel of a comfortable position for both of us.

"I did get propositioned," she said.

"Really?"

"Three times. Once by an older man who assured me his wife wouldn't be home for hours, and once by a woman who told me the same thing about her husband. You know, I'll bet those neighbors don't talk to each other, but they fuck each other in the afternoons."

"And the third time?"

"Well," she said, wrapping a lock of hair around her finger, "that was a younger guy, pretty handsome and in good shape..."

"Ally—"

"I didn't go in," she said, "but...I did give him my number, told him if he gets to town—"

"You can't do that in this business, Ally," I warned her. "Not when you don't know who you're dealing with."

"Oh come on," she said "don't tell me you never got laid while on the job—I mean, when you were younger."

That hurt, but I still didn't tell her about my blunder with Beth Munnings.

"You have!" she said, when I didn't answer right away.

"When I was younger," I said, thinking, a few days younger. "Okay, never mind. I might have come up with something."

"Ooh, tell me about it." She grabbed the chair in front of my desk and sat, her eyes shining. "Is it the partner? Or the wife?"

"Neither, I don't think," I said. "What I got came from his building."

I told her about my visit to Kessenger's building and my conversation with his neighbors.

"See?" she said when I was done. "More neighbors who don't talk, but fuck."

"Yeah, maybe."

"Well, the divorcee and the artist," she pointed out.

Yeah, I thought, and Beth Munnings with whomever. I wondered if Crazy Beth ever took a run at Kessenger?

"So what else did you get?"

"I put in a call to the morgue, a fella I know who does me favors." Favors I paid for. "He told me the M.E. found bits clay in Kessenger's head wound."

"Clay? So he was killed with...clay?"

"He was beaten with something made of clay."

"Like what? Pottery?"

"No," I said, "but maybe a statue."

"Well, were there statues there, at the scene."

"No," I said, "but there was, one floor down."

"What?"

"Where the artist lives," I said. "He paints, and he sculpts."

"So you think he killed him?"

"I don't know," I said. "I saw this statue in the neighbor's apartment, across the hall."

"The divorcee?"

I nodded.

"It had a chip in the base."

"The clay!"

I nodded.

"So then she did it?"

"That's the question," I said. "Is that the murder weapon, and did one of them do it?"

"So," she said, "how do we find out?"

"Well," I said, "we could just ask them."

I typed up my day's proceedings, and had Ally do the same. She suggested that she do it on my computer, because if she did it on hers and gave me a flash stick, my machine wouldn't be able to read it. I wasn't sure what all that meant, but I let her at my machine and she had it done in record time. Then she put both hers and mine went into the same file.

"So when do we start, boss?"

I looked up, saw Ally leaning against the doorjamb, again.

"Start what?"

"Askin' the questions."

"I thought I'd go back there tomorrow and talk to both of them."

"Do you think they'll tell you the truth?"

"I won't know until I ask."

"Let me go with you," she said. "Maybe we can figure out a way to get it out of them—or whichever one did it."

"Like how?"

"I'm goin' home," she said, "but I'm sure by mornin' you'll think of somethin'."

CHAPTER FORTY-TWO

I thought of something.

In fact, I thought of several somethings.

I thought of calling the police, giving them all I had, and leaving it to them. Then I rejected that plan. I was sure my employer, Griffith, would not approve of that.

So I considered going over to the building, somehow stealing that statue and then having it examined, forensically. I liked that idea, but I wasn't a burglar. I wasn't sure I could get it done.

Then I thought that all I needed from Devereaux, the artist, was a sample of the clay he used. If I gave that to the police, and they matched it with the bits in Kessenger's head, then I could leave the rest to them. Let them go in, get that statue, confirm it's the murder weapon, and then sweat both Devereaux and Miranda Cortez to see which one did it.

I left home and got to the office first. By the time Ally arrived, I had decided which way to go.

"You want me to what?" she asked from her now customary doorway position.

"Model."

"I'm not a model."

"I'm sure if you knock of Devereaux's door and he

sees you, he'll ask you in."

"What makes you think that?"

I thought about him asking Beth to pose.

"Because he's a man, and you're a pretty girl."

"What about my tattoos?"

"Show them," I said. "He loves colors."

"And then what do I do?"

"Get us a sample of his clay."

"What will you be doin'?"

"I'll be across the hall talking to Miranda Cortez," I said. "If anything goes wrong and you call out, I'll hear you."

"And do you have a gun?" she asked.

"I do."

"I've never seen you with it."

I opened a drawer and took out my .38 and belt holster. I never carried it, even though I had a permit. Now I clipped the holster to my belt and slid the gun home.

"There you go," I said.

"Well," she said, "I guess I feel a little safer."

"Ally, you don't have to do this," I said. "If he's the killer then this is dangerous. I'm just suggesting this because you want to learn the job, and because you did so well in White Plains."

"With those rich drips?" she asked. "They weren't dangerous, at all."

"What about the men who came on to you?"

"I can handle that," she said. "Don't you read the papers? Sexual harassment has been happening for years. But this...this is something else."

"Would you like me to come up with a different plan?" I asked.

"Are you kiddin'?" she asked. "This is gonna be

exciting." She pushed off the doorjamb, started to turn, then stopped and said, "So you think I'm pretty?"

CHAPTER FORTY-THREE

We went to Kessenger's Tribeca apartment building, up the stairs and stopped in front of the door.

"Are you ready?"

She was wearing a tank top that showed off all her tattoos, as well as her toned arms and shoulders, and trim figure.

"Ready as I'll ever be," she assured me.

I rang Miranda Cortez's bell, feeling fairly safe that she'd be there, and let me in.

"Who is it?"

"John Headston, Mrs. Cortez," I answered. "I have a few more questions about the Kessenger murder. May I come up?"

She didn't answer immediately, but suddenly the door buzzed open.

"Show time," I said, and we entered together.

We went up the stairs. I was hoping to get by the second floor without running into Beth, and we did. When we got to three, I kept my voice down.

"Stay on the stairs until I get inside, and then knock on his door."

"Right."

I knocked on Miranda Cortez's door and she answered

right away. Although it was even earlier than last time, she still had a martini glass in her hand. She was wearing an old-fashioned peignoir that made her look like a Robert McGinnis girl on a Richard S. Prather Shell Scott book cover.

"Come in, Mr. Headston," she said.

I stepped in and closed the door, peeking out first to see Ally come the rest of the way up the stairs.

She told me later what happened...

Ally stepped to Henry Lewis Devereaux's door and knocked. She said she had her story straight in her head and was rehearsing it.

Devereaux opened the door. She said he looked exactly as I had described, very wide and a few inches shorter than she did. But she said she could also see how some of his models might sleep with him. There was a sort of magnetism to him. I let that part of the story go.

"Well, hello," he said. "How did you get in here?"

"Somebody was comin' in just as I got here," she said. "I hope you don't mind..."

"Well," he said, leaning against the door, "I guess that depends, doesn't it?"

"On what?" she asked.

"On what you want, honey."

"I heard there was an artist livin' here who always needs models."

"And where did you hear that?"

"Ah...around the neighborhood."

"Babe, I'm gonna need a little better reference than that," he said. "A bar? A paint supply store?"

"Um...I hesitate to say this...but Beth told me."

"Beth?" He looked surprised. "Beth Munnings? My downstairs neighbor?"

"That's her," Ally said "I know you and she aren't, you know, friends or anythin', but I saw her in the laundromat—"

"Beth," he said, "Munnings."

"Yep."

He frowned and studied her.

"What'd she say, exactly?"

"You really wanna know?"

"I really wanna know."

"That you were a loser who invited her up to your place to paint her, and then you wouldn't even have sex with her. But she had to admit you were a decent painter." This was Ally ad-libbing.

Ally said he stared at her a few minutes, then smiled slowly and said, "Well, that sounds like Beth." He backed up and opened the door wide. "Come on in, doll."

While that was going on, Miranda Cortez once again led me to her expensive furniture layout. Along the way I eyed the statue again, to make sure it was still there. She offered me a drink. This time, I took it, looking to form more of a connection. If I was a younger, handsomer man I would have flirted. At my age I'd have to do it with liquor.

"Oh!" She looked surprised. "How nice. I actually hate drinking alone, probably because I do it so much."

"Really?" I asked, as she poured me a martini. "I would've thought Devereaux would be happy to come over and drink with you."

"Why?" she asked. "What did he tell you?" She handed me the glass.

"He warned me off," I said. "Said I better not try anything because you're his woman."

"Then he's delusional," she said. "I posed for him, we slept together, and that was the end of it."

"Really? Yesterday you made it sound like a relationship."

"Really?" She echoed. "How drunk must I have been? I suppose I made it sound like more than it really was. Truthfully, it was nothing more than a dalliance. It's all I'm capable of, right now."

"And yet he gave you that statue."

She looked over at it.

"Yes," she said, "I don't quite know why."

"Tell me something," I said, "when was the final time you saw Temple Kessenger?"

Her eyebrows went up.

"We're back to that again? And here I thought we were making progress."

"I'm still working on the case." I set my martini down, untouched, on the glass coffee table.

"Let me see," she said. "I think it was that morning, while we were getting our mail."

"Devereaux told me that Kessenger wasn't here long enough to get any mail."

"That might be true," she said, without even a blink, "but maybe he was just checking the mailbox, anyway."

I stood up and walked over to the statue.

"Do you mind?" I asked.

"You seem very interested in that thing, so go ahead," she said. "Be my guest."

I walked to the pedestal and lifted the statue from it. It was certainly heavy enough to have been a weapon. And then there was that chip...

CHAPTER FORTY-FOUR

Across the way Ally entered Devereaux's apartment, and the artist closed the door firmly behind her. Perhaps from habit he did not lock it.

"I like your tattoos," he said, running his finger down her bare back.

"Thank you." She stepped away from him and turned. "Does that mean you'd want me to model for you?"

"Are you looking for a paying model job?"

"Heck, no," she said. "I just wannabe immortalized."

He smiled. "Then allow me to immortalize you on canvas."

"Oh," she said feigning disappointment. "I was hopin' for somethin' more...substantial."

"Substantial?"

"Like concrete or...clay? I mean, you are a sculptor as well as a painter, aren't you?"

"Did Beth tell you that, too?"

"Well, yes." She told me she looked around then. "But I don't see any sculptures."

"Come with me to my studio." He put his hand out to her, and she took it. He led her to the other room, the one I had seen. She described the paintings all around them, and one on an easel.

"No statues?" she asked.

"They're in storage," he said.

"What about the clay?"

"Oh, I have some here, someplace," he said. "Why don't you get undressed while I get it ready."

"Undressed?"

"Well, yes," he said, I assumed you wanted me to sculpt you...nude."

Afterward, Ally said to me, "I'm a modern girl, Johnny, but I still wasn't anxious to get naked in front of him."

"What about his magnetism?" I asked.

"At that point he was startin' to get...icky. I mean, the way he looked at me."

But that came later...

She told me Devereaux left the room and she heard water running. She thought he was doing something with clay, so she decided to have a quick look around. As soon as she quietly opened the sliding door of a closet, she saw that it was haphazardly filled with clay figures of all sizes, as if he was trying to hide them there. I wondered if he could've been hiding them from somebody like the police. They had those clay pieces in an evidence bag, but did they even know that Devereaux was a sculptor?

"What are you doin'?" Ally heard from behind.

"I've got to tell you something," I said, hefting that statue in my hand. "Kessenger's head was bashed in. That's how he died."

"Oh," she said.

"Twenty-seven," I said, "that's how many times he was hit with something heavy and blunt."

"Are you saying—"

"This has a chip at the bottom," I went on, "and the medical examiner found clay chips in the head wound."

"Oh my God!" she said, going pale. "Are you saying...that's the murder weapon?"

"Could be," I said. "All we have to do is take it to a lab and look for traces of blood. No matter how well it was washed, if it's there the lab will find it."

"T-then what?"

"Then the police would have to figure out if Devereaux gave this to you and you killed Kessenger with it," I said, "or he gave it to you after he killed Kessenger."

"Oh my God!" she said again, this time sitting down and going as pale as death. "I think I'm going to be sick."

I waited, for either a confession, or an explanation.

"Do you think...could Henry have killed Mr. Kessenger with it, and then given it to me...to hide it?"

"When *I* was in his apartment and studio, I didn't see any sculptures."

"He usually has them all over."

"Then he probably hid them so when the police questioned him, they didn't see any."

"They don't know he's a sculptor?"

"I don't think the detectives would have that much imagination without proof right in front of their eyes," I said. "They heard he's an artist, and they're thinking painter. That's all they saw."

"So he hid all his sculptures, but this one he hid...here."

"When did he give this to you?"

"The day I heard Kessenger had been killed."

"Before you heard the news," I said, "or after?"

She thought a moment, took a quick gulp of her martini, emptying the glass. Then she put her glass down and picked mine up.

"Before."

Before I could ask another question, we heard a ruckus in the hallway, and I heard Ally yell, "Headstone!"

CHAPTER FORTY-FIVE

I ran to the door and threw it open in time to see Ally almost out the door of Devereaux's apartment, something in her hand. I saw his thick arm come around her neck and pull her back inside, and the door slammed shut.

I ran to the door, the statue still in my left hand, and grabbed the doorknob. Luckily, Devereaux was still leaving it unlocked for Miranda.

I pushed it open and ran in...

Ally told me later that Devereaux caught her snooping in his closet. When he asked, "What are you doin'?" she grabbed something, the smallest piece she could find, and then turned, holding it behind her back.

"I was just lookin' around," she said. "I couldn't help myself."

He walked past her to the closet and closed the door. She moved to one side, her hand still behind her back.

"Whatayagot there?" he demanded.

"Where?"

"Behind your back! What are you hiding?"

"Nothn'."

He grabbed for her, and that was when she bolted for

the door, yelling, "Johnny! Johnny! Headstone!"

I only heard the Headstone but that was enough.

Now, as I rushed into the room, she was wrestling with Devereaux, who had a lot of weight on her.

"Let her go!" I shouted.

He ignored me, and was bending her backward, trying to get what she had behind her back.

I rushed at him, hit them both with all my weight. It broke them apart. He staggered, and she fell to the floor. He looked at me, anger suffused his face with red.

"What the hell—she's with you?"

"She is." My shoulder hurt from hitting them.

He looked at my hand.

"What are you doin' with that?"

"I'm taking it to the police to check for traces of blood," I said. "You might want to turn yourself in and come downtown with me, Devereaux."

"Turn myself in for what?"

"You attacked me!" Ally said.

"You lied your way into my apartment and stole somethin'," he said. "I still wanna know what it is."

She glared at him.

Behind me I heard the door close.

"They know," Miranda Cortez said, and my heart sank.

I turned and saw that she was holding a small, silver automatic.

"Oh, shit!" Ally said. "Both of them?"

"Looks like it."

"She took something from my closet," Devereaux said.

"Well, get it from her!" Miranda ordered. "And get

that statue from him."

"You mean the murder weapon?" I asked, holding it up with my left hand. Her eyes went right to it. "If you want it, catch!" I tossed it to her.

Most women don't know what to do in a situation like that. A man would automatically reach out, probably one handed, to catch it. Her eyes widened as it flew toward her. She put both hands up to try to catch the statue, but the gun in her hand was in the way, so she fumbled and it fell to the floor, where it shattered. By the time she looked back at me I had my gun out, pointing at her.

Her eyes widened again and she started to bring her gun up, again.

"Mine's bigger!" I warned.

I backed up so I could stand next to Ally, who was still on the floor, and cover both of them.

"Drop it," I told her, "and let's talk."

CHAPTER FORTY-SIX

"All right," I said, after the gun hit the floor next to the pieces of what I thought was the murder weapon.

"That way," I said waving the gun. I wanted them to walk together to the sofa, where they sat side-by-side.

That done, I gave Ally a hand up. As she stood, I saw some more clay pieces on the floor.

"That was your sample piece," she said. "I sat on it."

"It can still be tested, and so can those. See if you can find two bags, will you? Let's keep the pieces separate."

"Right."

She went to find two bags. Miranda and Devereaux stared up at me. I noticed they were sitting with about two feet between them.

"So which one of you was it?" I asked.

"Which one?" Miranda asked.

"Which of you killed Kessenger?"

"Now wait a minute—" Devereaux snapped.

"I know," I said. "You're going to tell me you didn't kill him."

"That's right," Devereaux said.

"What makes you think we did?" Miranda asked.

"How about you coming into the room with a gun and saying, 'he knows?'" I asked. "That might've been a clue."

"That has nothing to do with the murder," she told me.

"Oh, really?" I indicated the pieces on the floor. "With that being the murder weapon one of you did it. My money was on him but now I think somehow you both did it. What I don't know is why."

Ally came back with two plastic supermarket bags, a broom and a shovel. She started sweeping up pieces.

"What are you going to do with those?" Devereaux asked.

"Give them to the police. They'll send them to the lab."

"I thought his wife killed him," Miranda said.

"Oh, sure," I said, "keep playing innocent."

"Well, she was here that day," she said.

"What?"

"His wife," Miranda said, "I saw her here the day he was killed."

"Inside the building?"

"No, at the front door," Miranda said. "I was getting the mail. I guess she was pressing his bell."

"And you didn't let her in?" I asked.

"Why would I?" Miranda asked. "I didn't know her."

"Did she see you?"

"You bet she did," Miranda said. "She flipped me off."

"Did you see her?" I asked Devereaux.

"What? No, I never saw her."

"Okay," Ally said, "I've got all the pieces."

Miranda and Devereaux were bugging me. They weren't acting like killers who had been caught.

"All right, here," I said, handing her my cell phone.

"Call detective Leon and tell him to get over here."

"Is that really necessary?" Devereaux asked.

"Well, since I think the two of you are murderers, yes, it is."

Ally moved off with the phone to one ear and her hand to the other.

"I told you," Miranda said, "we didn't kill him."

"What about the statue?"

"Henry gave it to me," she said, "that's true. But it's not a murder weapon."

"What about the chip in the base?"

"I did that," Devereaux said. "I stupidly knocked it against a wall. You saw how it shattered when Miranda dropped it."

"Why'd you give it to her and hide the rest of your pieces?" Ally asked, coming back.

"Well, I wanted her to have it," he said. "It would keep us...connected."

"The only way we're connected, Henry, is—" Miranda started, but then stopped short.

"How?" I asked. "In the killing of Kessenger?"

"Oh, you're impossible!" Miranda said. "I told you we didn't do that."

"Then why the gun?" I asked. I looked at Devereaux. "And why were you attacking Ally?"

"I was not attacking her, I was tryin' to find out what she stole."

I looked at Miranda.

"And the gun?"

"Oh, fuck you, Headstone!" she said. "Since you've already called the police, I'll talk to them when they get here." It didn't matter much at that point how she pronounced my name.

I backed away, keeping them covered. Ally came along with me.

"What do I do with these bags?" she asked.

"Just hold onto them, they're evidence." I looked at her. "Are you all right?"

"I'm fine," she said. "I just panicked when he started comin' at me."

"Speaking of which," I asked, "why did you yell out 'Headstone?'"

"Because I yelled Johnny and you didn't hear me."

"Well, I heard that."

She looked over at the two of them, still sitting apart.

"They don't look like lovers, or killers," she said.

"I know. That last part is what's bothering me."

I turned my attention back to the couple on the sofa, although they weren't sitting like a couple. But before I could say anything, Ally spoke up again.

"Johnny," she said. When I didn't answer she said, more stridently, "Headstone!"

"What?" I turned and looked at her, looked at what she was holding. "Where'd you find that?"

"In this bag," she said. "It must have been inside the statue I sat on."

I took it from her. A clear plastic bag with white powder in it.

"Look in the other bag," I told her.

She did, came out with a larger plastic bag with more powder that must have been inside the suspected murder weapon.

It didn't take a genius to figure out what it meant.

CHAPTER FORTY-SEVEN

"I think I'm getting this now," I said to them.

"About time," Miranda said.

"You two are moving drugs in this neighborhood, and Kessenger tipped to it. That's why you had to kill him."

"That again?" Miranda demanded. She turned her head and glared at Devereaux. "Tell him!"

He didn't look at me right away, but when he did, he started talking.

"I made a sale that day," he said. "The customer came to the door. I passed him the statue."

"That statue?" I asked, pointing to one of the bags Ally was holding.

He nodded, looking miserable.

"Then what?"

"I thought he left," he said, "but later I saw him come running down from upstairs."

"And?"

"H-he didn't have the statue, anymore." He stopped again.

"Keep going!" Miranda snapped.

"I was curious, so I went up. The door to Kessenger's place was open, so I went in. I—I found him there, dead, his head bashed in."

"With the statue?"

"That's right."

"And you took it?"

"Yeah," he said, "I figured if the cops found it, they might find the stuff inside. Or they might figure me for the murder, since I live downstairs and I'm an artist."

"You put all your sculptures in your closet," Ally pointed out.

"I knew the cops would talk to everybody in the building," he said. "When they came in, they didn't see any statues. That's what I wanted."

"But you didn't put this one in the closet," I said, pointing to the bag.

"No," he said, "I didn't even want it in my apartment, so I washed it off and took it to Miranda."

"And you put it on display," I said to her. "Why?"

"Who'd ever suspect a murder weapon was out in the open like that?"

"Why not just destroy it?" I asked.

They looked at each other.

"I get it," I said. "You might have been able to turn a dime by keeping it."

"How would they do that?" Ally asked.

"Blackmail's just a step up from drug dealing."

"But blackmailing who?" Ally asked.

"That's the question," I said, looking back at the couple on the sofa. They hadn't moved any closer together. They were partners, not a couple. "Who was the customer?"

"I don't know," Devereaux said.

"He wasn't a regular?"

"Well...yeah, but I don't know his name."

"Describe him."

"A big, heavy looking young guy with glasses," Devereaux said. "Big, but soft-looking. With a backpack. That's all I know."

The backpack part matched everybody, these days. But the rest...

"Like a Baby Huey type?" I asked.

He scrunched up his face. "Who's that?" He looked at Miranda, and she shrugged.

"How did he get in?"

"I buzzed him in."

"How did you know what he wanted?"

"They show up at the door and buzz. If they have the password I buzz 'em in."

"Password?" I asked. "Really?"

"It's the only way I let somebody in," he said, defensively.

"Do either one of you know how Kessenger found this building?"

"He said it was recommended to him by somebody."

Oh sure, I thought, by somebody who bought their drugs, here.

CHAPTER FORTY-EIGHT

Burger World was doing a brisk lunch rush...

I took a big chance, left Ally my gun so she could hold Miranda and Devereaux until the police showed up.

"Hey," Miranda had said, "does she know how to use that?"

"Not really," I said, "so if I was you, I'd sit still or she might accidently blow your head off."

When I left, they were staring at her with wary eyes...

The girl, Angie, was at her register, a pained look on her face. At the next register was somebody I didn't know, a skinny kid. I went up to her register, drawing hard looks from the people in line.

"Hey, Angie, is Mr. Woodley in?"

She looked at me, took a moment to recognize me, then said, "He's in his office. You know where it is."

There were too many people there for me to hop over the counter, so I went to the door. She had to take a moment away from her register to buzz me in.

"Hey—" the new kid started.

"It's okay, he knows Woodley," Angie told him.

He backed off.

As I walked back to the office, I drew a long look from Greg, the big kid Angie was going to have toss me out that first time.

When I got to the door the manager was staring down at his desk, his hand supported by his hands. I don't think he had any work, I think he was just silently bemoaning the fact that he worked there.

"Mr. Woodley," I said.

He looked up, saw me, and a relaxed smile came over his face.

"Oh Christ, an adult," he said. "I'm so tired of dealin' with kids."

"Can I come in?"

"Come on in, come on in," he said. "Close the door, if you want."

I did want, so I did.

"What's up?" he asked. "Any news on who killed Temp? There ain't been nothin' in the newspapers, yet."

"Can you tell me, how did Temp get along with the other workers here?"

He shrugged. 'Seemed to be okay. He wasn't here that long."

"What about the people on his shift? Angie, and Greg?"

"Well, you know, that's funny," Woodley said. "He got along pretty good with Angie, but Greg didn't seem to like that."

"Was Greg stuck on her?"

"I don't pry into my employees' business, but I think they went out a time or two. Now Temp, he was a nice, pleasant lookin' older guy, you know? And he treated her nice. She's kind of a sad girl, not happy with how she looks. I heard her complainin' one day to one of the other girls, sayin' she couldn't lose weight, and she didn't know how to use make-up, stuff like that."

"But that didn't matter to Greg, huh?"

"I guess not but look at the poor kid. He ain't the pick of the litter either, if you know what I mean."

"Kind of like Baby Huey, huh?"

"Hey," he brightened. "That big, yellow, baby cartoon duck."

"Right."

"Or are you talkin' about that soul singer from the sixties? You know, Baby Huey and the Babysitters? He died in nineteen seventy of an overdose."

"No, no," I said, "the first, one, the duck. That's who Greg reminds me of."

"Oh, yeah..." he said, shaking his head. "But that Baby Huey, the singer? I remember Curtis Mayfield wanted to sign him—"

"I don't remember him," I said, firmly. "I'm talking about Greg."

"What about Greg?"

I looked through the shoebox sized window on the door. Greg was putting together burgers and chicken sandwiches, but suddenly he looked over at the door, as if he could feel me watching him. I ducked back.

"Did he hate Temple Kessenger?"

"Of course not!"

"How can you be that sure?"

"I heard Greg telling Temp about that building Temp had his apartment in," Woodley said. "Why would he help him if he hated him?"

"Maybe the hate came later."

"But why—oh, you mean, because of Angie?" He laughed. "Mister, I think you got the wrong idea. Angie ain't the kinda girl one man would hate another man over. Or kill him? No."

"Well," I said, "I'm going to ask him about it. You mind if I use your office?"

"I guess not. But you're gonna see how wrong you are. Want me to get 'im?"

"That might be best."

He got up, opened the door and walked over to Greg. He spoke to him and jerked a thumb my way. Greg nodded, started walking my way, and then suddenly started running in another direction.

"Shit!" I snapped, hurrying from the office. "What'd you say to him?"

"Just that you wanted to talk to him about Temp."

"Is he going out the back?"

"Yeah but wait." He grabbed my arm. "You go out the front and make a left. He's gotta come down that alley. It's the only way out."

I turned and ran for the front door, Angie and some of the customers staring after me.

"What about my Around-the-World Burger?" I heard somebody yell.

I went out the front and turned left. After a few steps I came to the mouth of the alley Woodley had mentioned. As I did, I could hear Greg's footsteps coming toward me. When I turned in, I saw him, running toward me, but he was looking back over his shoulder for me.

Baby Huey or not, he was a big kid carrying a lot of weight, and he was running as hard as he could. Because I have a bit of a belly, I have a pretty good center-of-gravity. Nevertheless, I knew this was going to hurt.

I turned my shoulder and headed right for him. When he turned around and saw me, it was too late.

For both of us.

CHAPTER FORTY-NINE

They all came to see me at the emergency room: Ally, Detectives Leon and Stokes, the lawyer Griffith, and poor Angie.

Separately, of course.

Leon and Stokes were first.

"Hurt?" Leon asked, looking at my bandaged shoulder.

"Like hell," I said.

"Good! You should've called us first, and not gone after him, yourself."

"I did call you," I said. "That is, I had my assistant call you."

"The same untrained assistant you handed a gun to?"

"She's a smart girl—"

"That's neither here-nor-there," he said. "Headstone, this is the kind of thing that got you in trouble last time."

"Not quite—"

"If I yank your license it is!" he pointed out. I didn't bother pointing out that according to the Private Investigation and Security Act he couldn't yank my license, he could only recommend it. That would've just made him madder.

"I caught your killer," I reminded him, "and kept

you from prosecuting an innocent woman."

"Believe it or not, we," he pointed to himself and his partner, back-and-forth a few times, "would've come to that conclusion on our own. She would not have been prosecuted."

"Did you have the burger kid figured for it?"

He hesitated, then said, "No, but we were still investigating."

"What about the drug dealers I caught for you?" I asked.

"We gave them to the drug boys," he said. "They've been trying to find out who was pushing drugs in that area for months."

"Did they thank you?"

"They did."

"But you're not thanking me, you're berating me." I shifted position, trying to find one that didn't hurt. That's what happens when you get a displaced—not separated—shoulder and clavicle from colliding with Baby Huey.

"What about the kid?"

"He's in custody, and waitin' for a lawyer."

"Is he here? At the hospital?"

"He was luckier than you," Leon said. "They took him to the Tombs, for now."

Behind them, peering into the emergency room, I saw the lawyer, Griffith.

"My lawyer's here."

"You lawyered up?"

"No," I said, "he probably heard about it and came to see how I am. After all, I work for him." Ally must have called him. If she could. "What about my assistant?"

"Luckily," Stokes said, "she didn't shoot anybody, or

your license would be gone now."

"And she'd be in a cell."

"She's not?"

"No," Leon said, "she's waitin' outside to see you."

"Thanks," I said.

"For what?" Leon asked. "I still haven't said I won't go after your license."

"I know that," I said. "Thanks for her."

"She was just doin' what you told her to do," he said. "Now excuse us, we have to go and interview our suspect."

"Let me know what happens?"

Leon pointed at me. "You got a lot of nerve!"

He turned and stormed out. Stokes looked at me, shrugged, and followed him. Griffith watched them go, and then came in.

"How are you, Mr. Headston?"

"Battered and bruised," I said. "How's Mrs. Kessenger?"

"After your assistant called me, I called her. She wanted to come, but it would have taken a while. She wanted me to tell you she's sorry you got hurt, and she's grateful that you cleared her and caught the real killer."

"That was my job."

"And you're to be well paid." Griffith took a check out of his inside jacket pocket and passed it over. "That's a down payment. You'll get the same amount again when the killer is convicted."

I glanced at the check, approved of the number of zeroes on it, and stuck it in my shirt pocket, left-handed.

"And now," the lawyer said, "there are two ladies waiting to see you."

He turned and walked to the door, then turned back.

"If you have any trouble with those detectives and need a lawyer to keep your license, let me know."

"I will," I said. "Thanks."

He left, and moments later Ally came in, leading Angie, who had her head down.

"Are you okay, John?" Ally asked.

"I'm fine," I said. "Battered, but fine. How about you?"

"I thought they were gonna arrest me," she said. "They didn't like finding me there with your gun, and you gone."

"I know," I said. "They're not going to charge you."

"Oh," she said, "that's good. What about you?"

"That's still up in the air."

"Is your license in danger?"

"It's happened before," I said.

"Then why did you do it?" she asked. "Why not just call them and let them go to Burger World?"

"Because," I said, "it was my job. I was supposed to clear Mrs. Kessenger."

"And you did."

I nodded. I needed some more pain killers.

"Mr. Headston?" Angie said.

"Yes, Angie?"

"W-was this really about me?" she asked, hugging herself. "Did Greg kill Temp because he was j-jealous?"

"I'm afraid that's the way it seems now, Angie.," I said, "unless the police find out something else."

"Omigod." I couldn't tell if she was horrified, or secretly pleased.

CHAPTER FIFTY

I opened my eyes and wondered where I was. It was the pain killers. They threw me for a loop. But the hospital had only given me a week's worth, so I hadn't had any in a few days.

I looked at the doorway to my office and saw Ally standing there.

"What?" I said.

"You were telling me why that fella Greg told Mr. Kessenger about the apartment in that building," she said. "And then you nodded off."

I sat up straight in my office chair, tried to stretch. I wasn't bandaged anymore, but I was still pretty sore.

"Oh, right. Well, it seems he had a plan to kill two birds with one stone. He knew he bought his drugs there and knew there were apartments available. He also knew he could get into the building whenever he wanted to."

"And this was all because of that girl Angie? The fat one with the glasses?"

"Yes. Greg was in love with her, and he felt that Temp Kessenger was taking her away from him."

"But he wasn't."

"No," I said, "he was just being nice to her, and that's all it took to get the poor girl to fall in love with him."

"Wow," she said, "I don't see her inspiring that kind of passion, and I sure don't see him as a killer."

"Well," I said, "there's somebody out there for everyone. And I think everybody's got something they'd kill for. They just have to find it."

She was about to reply when the door opened and somebody walked in.

"Mrs. Kessenger just walked in," she said.

"Show her in," I said. "We don't have any coffee, right?"

"I don't do coffee," she said, and went to fetch the lady.

She showed Nancy Kessenger in and I started to stand.

"Don't bother, Mr. Headston," she said, getting my name right. "You look like you're still in pain."

"A bit sore, yes, ma'am," I said, settling back into the chair. "What brings you here today?"

"I wanted to give you this, personally," she said, handing me a check. It had at least as many zeroes on it as the check Griffith had given me.

"What for?" I asked. "You paid my bill, and your lawyer already paid me. Is this the promised bonus?"

"No, this is just from me," she said, "to show my gratitude."

It wasn't necessary, but I wasn't about to argue. I opened the center door of my desk and dropped the check in.

"And I still have a question," she added.

"What's that?"

"The one time I managed to talk to Temp, after he left," she reminded me, "he said that it was for my own safety."

I recalled that.

"Do we know what he meant by that?"

"No," I said, "and we may never know."

"Could he have been involved in the drug dealing?"

"You tell me, Nancy," I said. "Would there have been any reason for him to get involved in something like that?"

"I don't know," she said. "Boredom?"

"Was he bored?"

"Well, he obviously wasn't happy."

"As I said," I went on, "we may never know."

"Would you consider continuing with the case?"

"I'm afraid that I have some other things to deal with, first," I said, "like keeping my license. Let me get that done, and maybe later we can revisit this—if you're still interested."

"Very well." She stood up. "I have to go. I'm having lunch with Scott."

"Walcott?"

She nodded.

"I think he may offer to buy me out."

It sounded like Mrs. Kessenger was going to make out very well from all this. I walked her to the door and said goodbye, then turned to find Ally staring at me.

"Another check?"

"Yup," I said. "Come on, I'll buy you lunch and we'll talk about your future."

"Does the Headstone Agency have a future?"

"If it does," I said, "you'll be part of it, if you want."

"Like you said," she replied, "let's talk over lunch."

"What about that, John?" Ally asked me in the elevator.

"What about what?"

"Finding out why Kessenger thought what he did was protecting his wife," she said. "Don't you want to know what from?"

"That's one thing you'll have to learn about this business, Ally," I said, as the elevator stopped and we stepped out, "sometimes you just can't find all the answers."

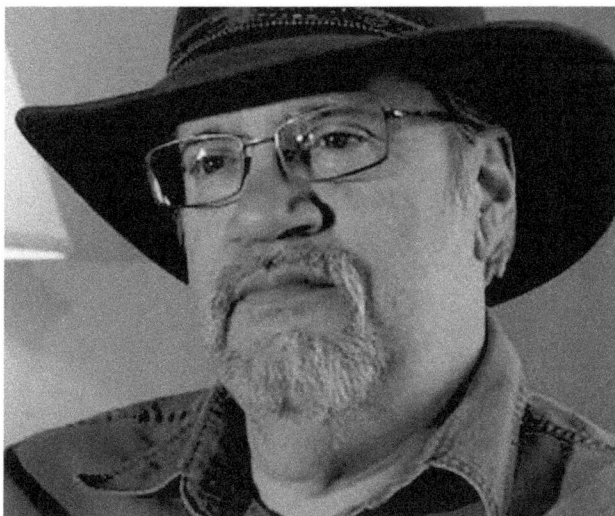

ROBERT J. RANDISI is the author of the "Miles Jacoby," "Nick Delvecchio," "Gil & Claire Hunt," "Dennis McQueen," "Joe Keough," and "The Rat Pack," mystery series. He is the editor of over 30 anthologies. All told he is the author of over 600 novels.

Randisi is the founder of the Private Eye Writers of America, the creator of the Shamus Award, the co-founder of Mystery Scene Magazine.

DOWN & OUT
BOOKS

On the following pages are a few
more great titles from the
Down & Out Books publishing family.

For a complete list of books and to
sign up for our newsletter,
go to DownAndOutBooks.com.

ALL DUE RESPECT   SHOTGUN HONEY

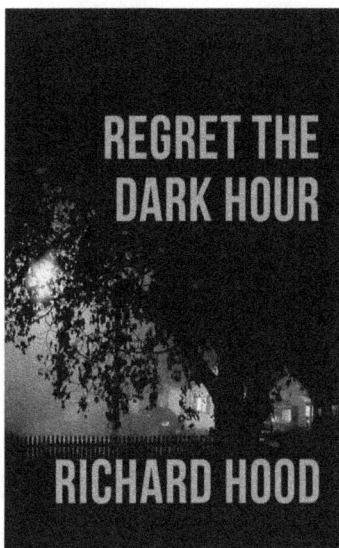

Regret The Dark Hour
Richard Hood

Down & Out Books
August 2019
978-1-64396-028-9

When Nole Darlen kills his father, the single resounding gunshot sets up a dark patchwork of memory and expectation. A tangled tale involving the dead man's wife, his neighbor, a desperado, and a grizzled muskrat-trapper. There is never any doubt about who killed Carl Darlen, but the story turns and weaves through the day of the murder and ends with a startling, dark, surprise.

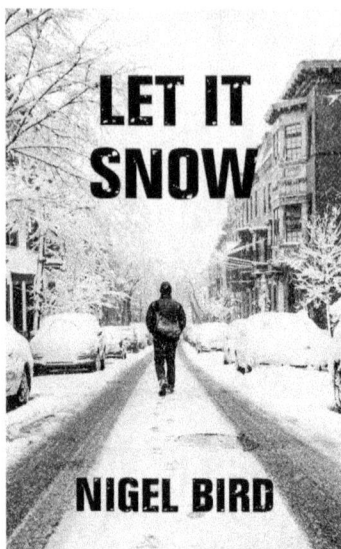

Let It Snow
Nigel Bird

Down & Out Books
November 2019
978-1-64396-047-0

A police officer is murdered while talking down a suicidal teenager. A rhino is killed at the zoo and has its horn removed. The biggest store in the city is robbed by a mannequin and record snowfall has created chaos within the police department.

As detectives seek the perpetrators of these crimes, they reflect upon their lives. Each of them needs to make changes. Not all of them know where to begin. It's going to be one hell of a Christmas.

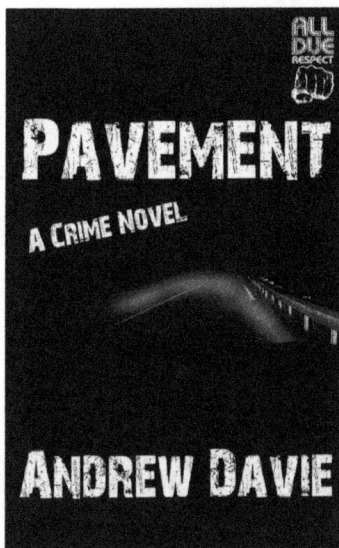

Pavement
Andrew Davie

All Due Respect, an imprint of
Down & Out Books
July 2019
978-1-948235-99-0

McGill and Gropper are unlicensed private investigators who operate out of a diner and do whatever it takes to get a job done. When a trucker attacks a prostitute, her pimp turns to McGill and Gropper for protection.

But taking the job means crossing dangerous and well-connected criminals who will stop at nothing to settle the score.

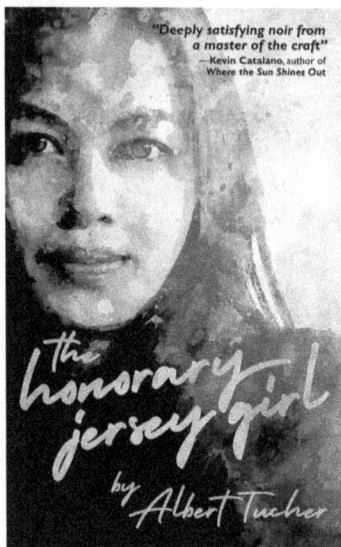

The Honorary Jersey Girl
Albert Tucher

Shotgun Honey, an imprint of
Down & Out Books
July 2019
978-1-948235-10-5

Because sometimes she needs to get tough…

On the Big Island of Hawaii criminal lawyer Agnes Rodrigues hires an ex-prostitute turned bodyguard from New Jersey to protect an innocent man.

Two Jersey girls are tougher than one, even if one is honorary.